BACKSTAGE
WALL STREET

AN INSIDER'S GUIDE TO KNOWING

WHO TO TRUST, WHO TO RUN FROM,

AND HOW TO MAXIMIZE YOUR INVESTMENTS

JOSHUA M. BROWN

New York ∘ Chicago ∘ San Francisco ∘ Lisbon
London ∘ Madrid ∘ Mexico City ∘ Milan ∘ New Delhi
San Juan ∘ Seoul ∘ Singapore ∘ Sydney ∘ Toronto

For Sprinkles, TJ, and the Nugget,

"The Home Team"

1 2 3 4 5 6 7 8 9 10 DOC/DOC 1 8 7 6 5 4 3 2

ISBN 978-0-07-178232-6
MHID 0-07-178232-X

e-ISBN 978-0-07178233-3
e-MHID 0-07-178233-8

This publication is designed to provide accurate and authoritative information in regard to the subject matter covered. It is sold with the understanding that neither the author nor the publisher is engaged in rendering legal, accounting, securities trading, or other professional services. If legal advice or other expert assistance is required, the services of a competent professional person should be sought.
—*From a Declaration of Principles Jointly Adopted by a Committee of the American Bar Association and a Committee of Publishers and Associations*

McGraw-Hill books are available at special quantity discounts to use as premiums and sales promotions, or for use in corporate training programs. To contact a representative please e-mail us at bulksales@mcgraw-hill.com.

CONTENTS

FOREWORD

Carnival Barker: *Step right up, Ladies and Gentlemen! Watch in amazement as the darkest secrets of American Finance are revealed. Behold the cast of characters, from the lowly dialer to the account opener to the retail broker—commission men all on the Street of Dreams. Be forewarned: you are about to partake of sights so horrifying, so monstrous, I urge any of you who are easily frightened or who experience nightmares, look away! Those of you with weak hearts or nervous disorders, for God's sake, put this book down and run screaming in the opposite direction!*

In the future, the latter half of the twentieth-century might very well be looked upon as the Golden Age of Finance. Sandwiched around the 1970s malaise were two of the most fantastic bull markets the world has ever seen. The first, the post–World War II expansion, ran for two decades, ending in 1966. It included the rebuilding of war-torn Europe and the reconstruction of Japan. It also saw the massive build-out of suburban America, with its interstate highway system and modern car culture. But it wasn't just the private sector that boomed; while suburbanites were busy keeping up with the Joneses, the space race had the military complex busy keeping up with the Khrushchevs. Mind you, these are not socio-economic criticisms. They are merely reminders of the investing themes of an era that helped to create trillions of dollars in wealth.

Following an inconvenient bear market, the next bull was even *more* glorious. The technology sector boomed, and with it, markets saw wild growth in the stocks of cellular, software, semiconductors, storage,

Internet, telecom, networking, and new media companies. So what if it all ended disastrously? There was a financial party to be had while it lasted.

And, oh, what a party it was: America was booming in the second half of the twentieth-century. As she grew, so too did her finance sector. In 1960, U.S. manufacturing profits totaled four times the size of finance profits. By 1980, earnings from manufacturing were merely twice the size of finance's. But finance slowly closed the gap, and by 1995 its profits were greater than those of the manufacturing sector. By 2005, the finance sector had swelled to 20.6 percent of U.S. GDP versus a mere 12 percent for manufacturing, according to Kevin Phillips, author of *Bad Money*.

America had become thoroughly "financialized." Formerly operating in the *service* of industrial economy, the financial services sector now *was* the U.S. economy. The tail no longer wagged the dog—it had taken over the entire wolf pack.

All of this financial paper didn't sell itself; it took fast-talking salesmen to jam $45 trillion in bonds and $25 trillion in stocks down America's throat. How that was done is what this book is about. It is unlike any other you may have read before. Countless tomes have looked at Masters of the Universe, the Big Swinging Dicks of Wall Street. This writing is not about them. Rather, it tells the story about lunch-pail guys—the average finance professionals, the stockbrokers, whose spiels sold America on a vision of high finance and fast money. These men and women worked the capital market trenches, slinging bullsh*t to get America to invest in herself—and pocket some commissions along the way.

The work before you is really two books in one. It is told from the perspective of a young man who jumps into the glamorous world of finance, only to discover the corruption that lay coiled at the heart of the brokerage business. It is a work of history as well as a morality play. If you pay attention as you read it, you will be both entertained and educated by the time you finish.

—Barry Ritholtz
January 2012

Broker-to-English Dictionary

A brief list of terms that will help you to enjoy this book.

Boiler room: A nonreputable brokerage firm that uses high-pressure telephone sales tactics, scripts, and an uneducated, amoral workforce to push dubious securities. The boiler room brokerage era saw its peak in the early to mid-1990s as the firms made markets in manipulated stocks and made secret payments to the brokers who pushed them.

Usage: "That firm is a real boiler room; all the brokers do is pitch penny stocks they make markets in."

Boutique: A term with two different meanings on The Street. Sometimes it is used to describe a firm that only services the wealthiest investors in the nation. Other times it refers to a firm that has a specialty or a specific area of expertise. Thomas Weisel and Hambrecht & Quist were boutique researchers and investment bankers to the technology industry, for example.

Usage: "ABC Petroleum is working with a boutique energy firm to both scout out potential acquisitions and invest the company pension plan."

Churning: Engaging in copious amounts of buying and selling for customer accounts with the primary purpose of generating commission revenue.

Usage: "I don't know why I'm being accused of churning just because I also buy a put option and sell a call option with every stock trade."

Cold slamming: Pitching cold leads you've never spoken with on a stock transaction.

Usage: "I was out of leads last night, but I cold-slammed California names until I got a new account."

Compliance: The "policeman" working for the firm that is somehow supposed to maintain order at the firm. If there is a more nonsensical setup in all of the working world, I'd love to be told of it. The compliance officer is paid by the firm's owners, who expect lots of revenue and profits, and yet he or she is in an oversight position and charged with making sure the salespeople generating these profits don't step over the line. The name of the game is allowing the brokers to push the envelope just far enough to keep the owners happy and the regulators at bay. Good luck with that.

Usage: "Compliance has been busting my balls over this option trading all month."

D and Bs: Dun & Bradstreet index cards with business owners' names and phone numbers on them. These were the leads that the big boys called with pride because of how wealthy the prospects were and how impossible they were to get through to.

Usage: "I worked my ass off today; got three D and B leads before the close."

Gross or G: Gross commissions. *G* is short for gross.

Usage: "Hopefully this stupid China Green Energy breaks out this month so I can sell it and do some G.

Independent: A firm that caters to brokers and advisors who are seeking both more autonomy in how they run their practices and a higher payout as a trade-off for the support they'd be offered by larger firms. The brokers who either go to an independent firm or start one can also be called *breakaways*.

Usage: "Going independent was a great choice . . . until I had to spend three hours on hold with tech support when my quote system went down."

Pay period: A four-week time frame dictated by the clearing firm being used. Brokerages pay their employees on the fifteenth of the month for their gross commissions earned during the prior month. The last day of each pay period is typically the Tuesday before the last Friday of the calendar month. On that Tuesday or the Monday before, you will all of a sudden see a flurry of trades get done so that the brokers can beef up their forthcoming paychecks.

Usage: "I gotta blow this Broadcom position out before the end of the pay period, or they're gonna flatbed my Jaguar right out of the parking lot."

Piker: A small-time broker, trader, or client. The *Oxford English Dictionary* defines *piker* as "a cautious or timid gambler who makes only small bets; a person who takes no chances; a 'poor sport' . . . a shirker." The origin of the term is not clear-cut. The most "American" explanation is that the term was coined during the

California gold rush. There was an area of Missouri, north of St. Louis, that hosted a large number of travelers headed west to try their luck mining for gold. Because these travelers came through or originated from Pike County, they became known as "pikers" during the course of their journey, in a similar way that travelers from Oklahoma became known as "Okies." Pikers in this context were characterized as frugal, cautious people who would avoid spending their money on anything, especially drinking or gambling.

Usage: "John is a real piker; he only bought 9,000 shares of that IPO this morning."

Popping accounts: Opening up new clients. The term is usually associated with pitching over the phone. Also referred to as *cracking accounts* or *popping a new bird.*

Usage: "If you can't pop at least eight accounts a month, you're gonna end up working at Schwab for $60k a year."

Producer: A broker who racks up large amounts of gross commissions on a consistent basis.

Usage: "Who cares what his clients' profit and loss statements look like; he's the top producer in the firm!"

Qualies: A qualified lead, which is what cold callers were paid to turn regular leads into.

Usage: "I'm psyched to get on the phones with this Activision pitch; I got a box full of qualies to call."

Regional: Originally, broker-dealers that were not based in New York and tended to cater to investors in their own hometowns. Examples include Raymond James, Dain Rauscher (now owned by RBC), Edward Jones, and AG Edwards (bought by Wachovia, which is now owned by Wells Fargo). The regionals have been disappearing into the folds of larger firms for years now, and the few remaining have been attempting to swim upstream in their offerings while also capturing the RIA trend.

Usage: "It's so nice to have a branch of a regional firm like AG Edwards in town so I can see my broker in person for updates on my portfolio."

The Seven: The Series 7 General Securities Registered Representative license. The Series 7 exam requires you to memorize enough useless information to get through a 6-hour, 250-question test. Most of the useful calculations one learns for the test are done by computers in the real world, and most of the ethics questions are obvious, making this the most pointless barrier-to-entry exam being given in the United States today. You should meet some of the cavemen I know who've managed to pass it.

Usage: "I just got my seven, yo! My license to print money!"

Wirehouse: A large firm with an interconnected network of branches and offices that share information and data. The origin of the term is from a time when a wire or cable connection was the only way for Wall Street prices and news to be sped to the far-flung branches of a brokerage firm. It has since come to mean a large and long-standing major firm, like Merrill Lynch. There are very few wirehouses left, but they've all gotten as large as they've ever been because of the shotgun wedding season of 2008–2009. These firms have also come to be called *bulge bracket* because they are chock full of so many departments and offer so many services.

Usage: "I went to work at a wirehouse because the firm had such a broad array of products and services to learn about."

Introduction:
Who Am I?

T echnically, I don't exist. I mean, I'm here writing these words, but on paper I am a perfect impossibility.

I am a former stockbroker and current investment advisor. I started as an independent while virtually everyone who has found success in my industry began their careers at large, well-known firms. I came in through the backdoor of the investing business, fought my way through, and learned everything through sheer force of will and the intellectual curiosity of an autodidact. This is important in that my training has not been informed by or infused with the traditional brokerage firm orthodoxy.

I am an artist and writer by nature, a financial professional by choice. I have no friends "at the top" or "on the inside," and I don't own a single one of those blue shirts with the white collars. Without having paid fealty to the traditional powers that be or having called in favors of any kind, I've used only my honesty, wit, and reputation to get to the Big Show. Thanks to the magic of the Internet, each day my market insights are read by thousands of people across the country and around the world. This is all without the marketing muscle of a traditional Wall Street firm and minus any PR or publicity help of any kind. I'm able to call it like I see it without fear of reprisal from a corporate hierarchy or the media establishment.

There is no such person as me in all of finance, and there has never been an investing book quite like this one; no one else could have possibly written it. No one who is currently working in the investment advisory or asset management business will ever say the things I am about to say or draw back the curtain the way I plan to. Most have too much invested in the mirage to tear at some of the scabs that surely itch them from time to time. I was never a part of that mirage, nor did it ever appeal to me. I was always a bit too "punk rock" to work at those vaunted banking institutions and hallowed halls of high finance—you know, the ones that unraveled like a ball of yarn right before your eyes during the credit crisis.

Rebels don't necessarily survive on The Street, and they almost never rise to a position of any influence or prominence. The fact that someone like me has—and is articulate enough to tell of the things I've seen—well, let's just say they'll never see me coming. So when I tell you that I don't exist, let me assure you, this is no exaggeration. To call me a unicorn would be an understatement; I am a unicorn that can swim and speak fluent Portuguese.

There is a financial services industry facade that has been built on the premise of precision, an artifice that's been decades in the making and billions of dollars in the marketing. The implication of this perpetual campaign is that "there's a right way to invest, and only we are privy to its mechanics, we'll take it from here."

On The Street, our back tests are our blueprints, mathematical proof positive of "what works."

Our colorfully rendered charts and graphs are the stained glass windows beckoning you into the Cathedral of Exactitude, the Church of Certainty wherein all the secrets of money management are guarded by the Chartered High Priests of Financial Acumen.

But let's keep it real. Behind the construction of every strategy, every product, and every program that has been sold to the investor class, there are very human people making very human decisions. Precision may be the intent, but at the end of the day we are all just people, standing behind big-kid lemonade stands doing the best we can. Some of us use better-quality ingredients than others or are more adept at attracting potential customers. Some of us are meticulous in our process, while others are more willing to adapt, selling hot chocolate when the season's turn eradicates demand for our original icy offering.

The truth is, there is no more precision in financial services than there is in medicine or architecture or computer science. Things go wrong, people act emotionally, and not everyone has the best intentions at all times. I have several thousand headlines dating back to when stock trading first took place under the Buttonwood Tree to prove this.

Even in the aftermath of one of the worst financial crises in world history, a crisis that many believe is still ongoing, the Precision Myth enshrouds every communication from the investment management business. No one has done more in the last two years to shatter this Precision Myth than I have.

I've written thousands of articles and blog posts for my own site, *The Reformed Broker,* and for media outlets like CNN, the *Wall Street Journal, Forbes,* the *Faster Times,* the *Christian Science Monitor,* Yahoo! Finance, and CNBC. I've done hundreds of television appearances, web videos, and radio shows. I've been cited and quoted by the likes of Reuters, Bloomberg, the *Financial Times,* and several foreign newspapers whose names I don't feel like misspelling here. I've been called "pot-stirring and provocative" by *Barron's,* an "iconoclast" by *Research Magazine,* and "the Merchant of Snark" by the *New York*

Times. The message I've tried to convey throughout is that there is no "system." We all are fallible no matter how smart or rigorous we may be, no matter how sophisticated our process. Most importantly, investing precision itself is a fallacy, and those who make forecasts with certainty are doomed.

THE PRECISION MYTH IN PRACTICE

One of the main differences between those who work in the money management industry and their customers is that the former are trained never to allow the latter to catch even a glimpse of doubt. While this is obviously disturbing, there is also something oddly admirable about that near-universal dedication to the Precision Myth among financial professionals.

"Pick up those phones, people, and let them know it's going to be OK." But what if some of the professionals themselves are unconvinced that things will be OK? Is this permissible? Is there room in this line of work for even a molecule of indecision or doubt?

"Be right, be wrong, but have an opinion." Is this a logical line of thinking or a spate of nonsense worthy of only the most grotesque character from the pages of a Lewis Carroll story?

"Hold their hands, be reassuring. This is what they're paying us for." You'd be amazed at how true this statement actually is, particularly in the midst of crisis. But what good is offering my hand to an investor if I believe, as he does, that we are both about to tumble off a cliff? It turns out that to that investor, my grasp is more important than oxygen itself, I have come to learn.

"They're not buying the steak, they're buying the sizzle." This made sense in the early days of my career, as most of the men who delivered this line looked as though they lived upstairs from a steakhouse and the restaurant paid them rent in thrice-daily steak dinners.

"We're in the business of selling intangibles, these are only pieces of paper after all . . . we sell the potential for profits, not the profits themselves." When you are selling "goods" to a client in the form of investment products, can you also be providing "services" to that client in good faith? The industry's regulations do not yet stipulate that you have to.

The civilians don't often get wind of these types of statements; the attitude and thought process behind them somehow never make it into the marketing.

ROWERS IN THE GALLEY

Hundreds of thousands of people currently work in the financial services industry in various capacities, many of whom will not be discussed here. In *Backstage Wall Street*, we narrow our focus on the customer-facing and marketing part of the industry. We concern ourselves with the men and women on the benches of the galley who create that daily veneer of investment management precision with every stroke. Lifting and dipping their oars, these are the rowers who keep the ship gliding smoothly in the eyes of the observers ashore.

I want to emphasize that these are good people by and large, doing what they can within the confines of their career choice and under the limitations imposed by the lizard brains we've all inherited. I may be a muckraker and a satirist, but I am by no means a heartless one. It's never easy separating one's disdain for an organization from the acknowledgment that within there are likely to be wonderful people who are caring, hardworking, and conscientious. Some of my very best friends and smartest acquaintances work for banks, brokerages, and the like. The late comedian George Carlin had a pragmatic way of making this distinction that I have adopted for myself. In the 1970s, he said, "I love people, I hate groups. People are smart, groups are stupid." Anyone with a family member involved in pet causes, local politics, professional sports fandom in Philadelphia, or something along those lines can certainly relate to this rationalization.

So no, we do not despise the subjects of this book's focus individually, though we may at times despise the practices and institutions they represent. I don't believe that the industry on the whole is inherently good or evil; I simply believe that its very existence is ineluctable. If the World's Oldest Profession is prostitution, then surely its second oldest is financial advice. Whenever money is earned, after all, there is a desire for the optimal preservation and utilization of that capital . . . be it animal pelt, grain, or stone weaponry. And besides, without all those financier Master of the Universe types, who's going to keep all those prostitutes busy?

The methods of compensation, the means of delivering wisdom, and the instruments of investment themselves may evolve, but there will always be an advice business for as long as there is money. And as long as there is an advice business, there will be people who earn their living at it. The people toiling below deck are to be commended for the courage it takes to pit themselves so willingly against such unpredictable occupational hazards as economics and finance. They should also be feared to some extent, for they—we—must be certifiably mad.

LIGHTS, CAMERA, FINANCE!

Wall Street is everywhere. Its marketing reach is limitless. According to *BusinessWeek*, the securities industry spends $15 billion a year advertising more than 14,000 different funds, 8,000 stocks, and an unknowable number of bonds and fixed-income instruments. To put that number in perspective, the alcohol and beer industry spends only $2 billion per year. There isn't a televised sporting event in the country that doesn't count a financial firm as a sponsor. There isn't a newspaper in the nation that doesn't count on at least some ad revenue from a fund company, brokerage, or bank. Most people simply fast-forward the commercials and flip over the ad pages without stopping to pay attention. If you've seen one brokerage ad, you've seen every one of them.

There is a common theme that runs through almost all investment marketing: "We know what we're doing in the market."

This would be fabulous if true; unfortunately, by definition it's impossible. A market is made up of buyers and sellers, both of whom believe they are on the right side of a given purchase or sale. They cannot both be right. Now we can take a detour and say that a buyer may be wrong short term but absolutely right long term, but the advertising we're discussing doesn't merit quite that degree of nuance. After all, what brokerage ads are meant to convey is that the firms cannot possibly be wrong because even when they are wrong, they are still right. Speaking of Lewis Carroll, somewhere the Red Queen is smiling down on this ubiquitous marketing message with immense, almost maternal pride.

Well, pardon me for acting as the wrench that fate has sent to be thrown into the works, so to speak. Excuse me for having heard (and written) every pitch and every sales rap that's ever been uttered. Forgive me for having made the decision to begin blogging as a human being, and by doing so, to begin pulling back the curtain.

Not only have I seen these films before, I've been on the studio back lot during their production. I've met the director and have hung out with the actors in their trailer between takes. I know where the makeup artist parks her car each morning and which screenplays are most in need of a rewrite. I know what dishes craft services is putting out for lunch and which sequels were only green-lit because the studio knows you're going to buy a ticket.

Wall Street has long incorporated the most effective showbiz techniques into its repertoire. And while you may have gotten a peek backstage before, what I'm about to show you will be entirely new and somewhat revelatory.

Welcome to the reality behind all the false glamour, contrived accuracy, and manufactured confidence. Welcome to a world where institutions feign perfection and human beings pretend an omnipotent mastery over the random and uncontrollable.

This is your guided tour.

PART ONE

THE PEOPLE

*A stockbroker is someone who invests your
money until it's all gone.*
—Woody Allen

*The game taught me the game. And it didn't
spare the rod while teaching.*
—Jesse Livermore

*And when my situation ain't improving, I'm trying
to murder everything moving.*
—Jay-Z

1

Other People's Money

Fred Schwed opened his 1940 classic book, *Where Are the Customers' Yachts?* with the following introduction:

> *"Wall Street," reads the sinister old gag, "is a street with a river at one end and a graveyard at the other." This is striking, but incomplete. It omits the kindergarten in the middle, and that's what this book is about.*

Fred chronicled the madness of the 1920s and 1930s boom-bust cycle hanging out as a customer in the brokerage houses of Wall Street. He managed to stick around long enough for the 1950s' bull run before passing away in 1960. Had he the ability to come back now, I believe he'd be highly amused at the fact that this Wall Street

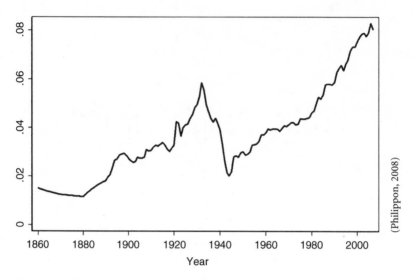

(Philippon, 2008)

Figure 1.1. *GDP Share of Financial Industry*

"kindergarten" has since become the dominant power in virtually every facet of our daily lives.

According to the research of NYU Stern professor Thomas Philippon, the financial sector's share of U.S. GDP has more than tripled from when Schwed was writing in 1940 (see Figure 1.1). The economic resources we spend on commercial banking, investment banking, private equity, and insurance have grown from 2.5 percent of the total pie to a whopping 8.3 percent through 2006. Philippon notes that each surge in finance's share of annual GDP over the years has been commensurate with an important societal advance, like the heavy industrial growth of the late 1800s, the electricity and automobile revolutions of the 1920s, and the IT spending explosion that began in 1980. But by the turn of the millennium, the financial services sector began to grow purely for the sake of growing. There was little benefit to the rest of the nation as financial engineers found more and more ways to keep finance itself in a self-perpetuating boom phase. And we know what happened next: the repo men came and took your no-money-down, canary yellow Hummer right out of the driveway of that house you didn't really belong in.

One of the most obvious signs of this metastasizing in the financial sector could be seen in the employment tallies at the banks and real estate firms themselves. We're talking about over 7 million people whose jobs consist mainly of pushing your money back and forth, up and down, in and out. The industry's sheer size may have gotten a bit silly, but its compensation policies are now bordering on slapstick. In 2008, Philippon told the *Wall Street Journal* that "in 1980, finance workers made about 10 percent more than comparable workers in other fields . . . by 2005, that premium was 50 percent." No wonder people don't want to do anything else with their lives other than flip houses, trade stocks, and sue each other.

Fueling much of this boom in revenue, profits, employment, and compensation growth for the finance industry was the global brokerage sales force. These are the men and women who go to work each day to find a buyer for every product and service that Wall Street can dream up. Heaven forbid they should take a month off; one can just picture the skyscrapers toppling and airplanes dropping out of the sky.

Brokerage firms are often referred to as "shops" by those who work in them, and this is because, like any other type of shop, the goal is to sell stuff to people. A brokerage firm, or broker-dealer, is in the business of facilitating the buying and selling of financial products, instruments, and, nowadays, advice.

This is not necessarily a bad thing.

Human beings in general are innumerate, and the vast majority of Americans don't have the time or interest to learn the basics of investing, let alone the intricacies.

There was a popular recent study that polled teenagers from around the world as they exited a mathematics exam. In terms of their scores, it should come as no surprise that the American students finished somewhere in the middle of the pack compared with their global counterparts. But when asked about how they *thought* they had done, it was those same average-scoring American kids who led the survey in self-confidence about their own performance. This is both wonderful and terrifying at the same time. There is an indomitable beauty in this uniquely American attitude, but unfortunately, overconfidence and middling numerical savvy do not exactly align well with successful investing. This is why there will always be a need for investment advice and a role for those who give it professionally.

The truth about civilian investors is that, in the aggregate, they will almost always enter and exit stocks and bonds at the wrong time. This has been proved over and over again, whether we're looking at mutual fund inflows and outflows, 401(k) contributions, retail brokerage firm margin debt, or almost any other gauge that tells us what the average investor is up to. Nothing makes this point more starkly, however, than a look at extreme readings in sentiment polls like the one produced by the American Association of Individual Investors (AAII).

The AAII conducts a weekly sentiment poll to track the mood of retail market players. The historical averages for this highly regarded poll are roughly 39 percent bullish, 30 percent neutral, and 30 percent bearish. As the S&P 500 was putting in its high-700s bottom in late 2002 and early 2003, this survey was repeatedly flashing extreme bearish sentiment readings of over 50 percent (see Figure 1.2).

An even more telling example of this phenomenon took place during the bottoming process that followed the credit crisis. During the week of March 5, 2009, the S&P was sitting at about half the level of its 2007 bull market peak; it had been gruesomely poleaxed in half

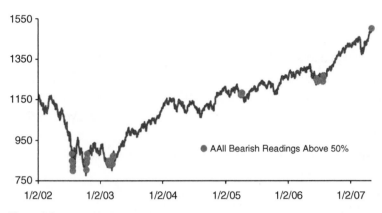

Figure 1.2. *S&P 500: 2002–2007*

over the course of the prior 15 months. The AAII sentiment survey that week reported 18 percent bulls and 70 percent bears—a record-breaking measure of bearish sentiment that has never been seen before or since. *Spoiler Alert:* The S&P 500 would put in an actual bottom at 666 four days later. It would be up 20 percent within a matter of months—quite an inconvenient rally given that most people had been cleared out of their stocks by this time. Within 24 months the market would achieve a double off its March 2009 low, this double happening while a huge swathe of investors watched from the sidelines in disbelief.

While there are those who have found success investing on their own, the great majority of what we'll call "ordinary" people would be better off getting some help. This is certainly not to say that they should take and pay for the advice of just anyone who is willing to give it!

In the aggregate, the professionals are not much better at picking market bottoms; sentiment on Wall Street matched the panicky mood on Main Street during this period for the most part. But there was a difference between how the pros and most individuals reacted to this widespread pessimism that is very important to understand. When it became more likely that we had seen the worst of what Mr. Market had in store for us, the pros were more willing to pull the trigger and begin buying stocks again, while many civilians simply couldn't snap out of their trance until much later. To some extent, you could argue that the brokerages had an extra incentive to boldly pull the trigger—you can't charge commissions to an account that is sitting in cash. This is a fair point, one that we'll be discussing at length a bit down the road.

In the spring of 2009, I was managing a branch office and 30 stockbrokers, and they in turn were working with thousands of retail accounts. The brokers were every bit as gun-shy about committing capital as their customers were in the post-Lehman wastelands of the stock markets. But they did it anyway because it was the only thing you could do when the market has erased 15 years' worth of forward progress for the major indexes. The best guys I know from firms all over The Street kept buying, even when their initial forays resulted in immediate drawdowns, even with the clients holding their hands over their eyes, not daring even a peek.

I do not wish to make the point here that professional investors have proved themselves to be naturally adept timers of the market. What I am attempting to convey, however, is that professionals tend to be less emotional. Part of that stems from the fact that professionals are managing other people's money, and so they have that luxury of emotional detachment. Another part stems from their being desensitized to a lot of the volatility by the sheer fact that they live with it 32½ hours a week while the markets are open. Psychologists do not psychoanalyze themselves when they find themselves overwhelmed; they have their own shrinks on speed dial. An outside, detached perspective is needed sometimes, especially when it comes to money— one of the most emotionally intense aspects of our lives.

The truth is, it is only at market peaks that most ordinary Americans get really interested and engaged in the stock market. They build up a knowledge base and a passion for investing just in time for the next crushing bear market to begin. In fact, the last bull market ended in 2000, just as stock market investing had supplanted baseball as the national pastime. Then the new national pastime became real estate, and a discussion about stocks got you laughed out of the room. This lasted until 2007 when stocks staged a credit-related echo-bull market, topping out before ultimately following the housing bull market right off a cliff.

Fortunately, America's new pastime is neither baseball nor stocks nor housing. Rather, it is checking our phones for e-mails; brushing our Cheetos-stained fingertips across them as though we're conducting the world's tiniest symphony. By which I mean we might be somewhat safe for a while.

By highlighting these recent financial manias and denigrating the participation of retail investors at their peaks, I am by no means inferring that if those investors had just listened to the brokerage industry, they'd have been fine. In fact, quite the opposite. Brokerage firms exist to cater to the whims of investors. When those whims tend toward speculation in a given investment theme, the brokerages roll out the drawing boards and begin cooking up products and strategies to satiate those appetites and meet the demand head-on.

This is all to be expected; once again we are talking about *shops*—retail stores that happen to sell intangibles. You wouldn't fault a Korean grocer for displaying a variety of different apples the day after Oprah tells her audience that they are to eat three apples a day, would you?

The bottom line is that the brokers need something to sell. This product creation mechanism takes a "story" that investors will be receptive to and turns it into profits for the brokerage firm.

We are also not talking about a phenomenon that is in any way unique to Wall Street. Hollywood understands this concept very well, and the vast majority of films that make it to the production stage do so as a result of what the studios believe will sell to audiences. Sequels are rarely about an artistic desire to continue the story. They are about a financial desire to continue the story. There is nothing inherently wrong with this, as it makes moviegoers happy to revisit characters and worlds they love. But these films are not art for the most part, and they are in many ways unnatural, forced creations of commerce.

Every once in a while something is produced in Hollywood for its artistic merits alone, but even in these cases a hard charger like Harvey Weinstein will come in as a distributor to push the film. No one should be surprised by this; the art versus commerce debate has been raging since the first Greek playwrights complained about the gyro vendors traipsing up and down the amphitheater's aisles during a production of *Antigone.*

Hollywood's business-savvy players will make sure that even if they end up with an art film that bombs at the box office, there will still be profits to wring from it. This is the reason there are so many movies up for awards each year that no one you know has actually seen. The studio says, "Well, we may as well go for some prestige and push this for a Golden Globe; at least we can juice the DVD sales and cable rights that way."

In much the same manner, the brokerage firm does not require a "big hit" in order to make money. The selling concessions or fees in the vast majority of products accrue to the seller of the product regardless. The success or failure of a particular instrument can only be judged over the long term. Should it be judged to have been subpar, no matter, because the commission's already been paid long ago. This calculation is at the very heart of the business model.

The brokerage business has always been a very "heads we win, tails somebody else loses" proposition. The client has the financial risk; the broker has the "reputational" risk. The nature of selling financial products and intangibles (like the prospect for earning profits in a given investment) is such that a victory justifies all manner of fees and a loss is the market's fault.

How does this continue year-in, year-out? Well, it's not exactly like they've stopped making new people in this country (it's way too fun a manufacturing process), and so the brokerage firm rarely runs out of new investors to sell things to.

2

In the Beginning . . .

At the end of the 1700s, European-style bourses and trading centers were beginning to coalesce in major cities like Boston, Baltimore, and Philadelphia. In lower New York, trading began down by the wall that Peter Stuyvesant had built during the previous century as a defensive barrier for the island of Manhattan (or New Amsterdam). This location would come to be known as Wall Street, the *financial capital of the world*. The activities and ethos of this otherwise insignificant street would go on to transcend geography: Wall Street is no longer just a physical place; it is its very own globally recognized culture, and it can exist anywhere someone is engaging in stock or bond wheeling and dealing. In fact, anywhere you go in this world, you can use the term *The Street* and businesspeople will know exactly what you're referring to.

I came up in the business working "on Wall Street" even though I never worked in a building with a physical Wall Street address. But my own story begins in the relatively recent past. To understand how Wall Street became part of the broader culture, we need to start at the very beginning.

By 1790, there was already a healthy amount of land speculation and bond trading in the colonies, but stock trading was first starting to come into its own. There were two types of traders running around Wall Street in those days, the auctioneers who set the prices for securities and the dealers who bought and sold them among one another. The broker-dealer system of the modern age has its roots in exactly this arrangement.

The "history repeats itself" crowd will be delighted to hear that, even in that early era, the auctioneers were constantly manipulating and rigging their securities prices. In fact, the first bailout occurred when a New York merchant named William Duer blew himself up with leveraged speculative positions and Alexander Hamilton himself had to step in to help all the parties unwind their exposure. Some things will never change.

By the mid-1800s, railroad shares and shipping stocks were all the rage in the unregulated marketplace that came to be known as Wall Street. In typical boom-bust fashion, the Civil War's aftermath and its effect on securities markets began bankrupting some of the very first brokerage firms and trading concerns, among them Jay Cooke & Co, Clark, Henry Clews, and Fisk & Hatch.

It wouldn't be until the 1890s that Charles Dow's namesake index (the Dow Jones Industrial Average) would be published on a daily basis by the *Wall Street Journal*. Dow was both founder and editor of the *Journal*, and his trackable indexes (there was also one for transportation stocks) made the daily goings-on of the stock market more accessible to outsiders. This, combined with the war bond efforts of the World War I era, had a seductive effect on the new, emerging middle class. Over the next two decades, participation in markets began to blossom to match the new era of consumption and consumerism that had taken hold of the American populace. Not coincidentally, it was at this time that the banks began acquiring brokerages and dealers in order to begin selling stocks to their new clients—the everyday American citizen. What was once a market for traders, robber barons, and the speculative few had become more welcoming to the newly moneyed East Coast "civilian."

The response to various war bond sales through 1916 and 1917 kicked down the door for the sale of corporate bonds, a gateway drug if ever there was one. In fact, the brokerage houses helped sell these war bonds with zero commissions (or barely discernible profits), essentially using them as a loss leader to establish relationships with millions of individual investors who simply hadn't existed before then. Once the brokerage houses had war bond buyers, converting them to corporate bond buyers would be a cinch. According to Charles Geisst's A History of Wall Street, there were only 350,000 individual investors in the bond market in 1917, but by 1919 that number had ballooned to 11 million! As these bonds matured, the principal was only headed in one direction—toward whatever securities the brokerage houses wanted to sell next.

By the 1920s, the securities markets were booming, and the business of business had exploded from the corner of Wall and Broad, radiating outward across the country along with our burgeoning communications capabilities. Investors were hungry for investments in radio, telephony, automobiles, and Florida real estate. The brokerage firms would find a way to satiate that hunger if it killed them.

When the party ended in October 1929, that blessing of communication turned into a curse. Wirehouses were able to transmit the horrible headlines and prices as quickly as they had previously been able to spread the decade's joy. People were to learn of their ruin instantaneously. The great irony of the Crash of 1929 was that the brokerage firms themselves had weathered it in fine form—not one of the major brokers of that era was bankrupted or forced to liquidate. They had been able to purge their inventories ahead of all the sell orders coming in from customers in the time-dishonored tradition that we now call "front-running."

The crash and resulting Great Depression brought serious regulation and reform to the Wall Street free-for-all that had enabled the bankrupting of half the nation. There was little vocal opposition to the new rules coming from the brokerages, as many of them were attempting to avoid being blamed outright for the mania and resulting chaos. I'll pause here to allow you to remember that we're talking about the 1930s and not the events of 2008. Quite an eerie coincidence, huh? OK, let's continue.

The Depression only put the American investor on the sidelines temporarily. Now that the public had a taste for stocks and bonds, it would be but a matter of time before people would come back. And you better believe that they were going to need some brokers at the ready to take their orders when they did. Many of the brokerage giants we know today are the very firms that were standing ready for exactly that call.

Charles Merrill and Edmund Lynch, both born in 1885, become acquainted out of necessity in 1907—they each needed a roommate for the YMCA on 23rd Street in Manhattan. Seven years later Merrill would open a brokerage firm on Wall Street, the ambitious optimist ready to carve out his piece of the expanding securities explosion. Lynch, his cautious and risk-averse friend, would soon join him as a partner in the firm.

They initially focus on investment banking and spin the brokerage off into a subsidiary that Merrill reacquires when it runs into trouble during the Depression. Combined, the brokerage and investment bank make for a juggernaut. Unlike Morgan Stanley and other investment banking firms, Merrill has a built-in brokerage sales force. This means that Merrill can underwrite and place its own securities directly with the firm's brokerage customers. This potent combination helps the firm become one of the most well-known and powerful brokerages in the nation.

Eddie Lynch dies in 1938, but Charles Merrill will live until 1956. That same year, the firm they had created together takes the Ford Motor Company public and has its first year of over $1 billion in underwriting revenues. I should remind the reader that in the 1950s a billion dollars was still real money, not just the amount that we now automatically pay every first-year analyst at Goldman Sachs. Anyway, a year later Merrill Lynch goes on to become the largest retail broker in the world; by the 1960s it has 121 offices, many of them staffed with Irish American brokers, earning the company its unofficial nickname, the "Catholic firm."

The company explodes into the 1970s, brimming over with innovation and ambition to spare. This is ironic because at exactly that time, many retail investors began abandoning stocks and bonds due to an ongoing bear market and a stagflationary economic environment. Merrill comes public in 1971, the first Big Board member firm to trade on the Big Board itself. It is now operating in 40 countries around the world and has adopted the famous bull logo along with the tagline "Bullish on America." The firm ends up having so much customer cash sloshing around in its brokerage accounts that it invents the Cash Management Account in 1977, the world's first money market fund. Many brokerage firms have come and gone over the years, but none have so completely epitomized the maturation and evolution of the industry alongside its ever-growing customer base.

In the meantime, paralleling the ascendancy of Merrill and Morgan and Smith Barney, a new and less Wall Street–centric type of brokerage firm is incubating. The "white-shoe" firms would not have the American investor (and that money) all to themselves for much longer.

In 1943, lawyer Edward C. Johnson II takes over an investment fund called Fidelity and starts the complementary Fidelity Management & Research Company (FMR) to manage its holdings. Johnson is a staunch advocate of research and the belief that investors could (and should) outperform the market as a whole if they worked hard and knew how to analyze stocks. He runs the company for 25 years and is known simply as "Mr. Johnson" everywhere he goes. The company sticks to its plan to remain private, even as every one of its competitors over the years does an IPO. Mr. Johnson wants to be impervious to short-term pressures and maintain control in the face of those regular storms that play havoc with markets and public companies. In 1973, Mr. Johnson's son Ned takes the reins and leads the newly formed FMR holding company further into the brokerage business and beyond.

That same year, an innovative renegade by the name of Charles Schwab raises $100,000 in seed money from his uncle and changes the way stocks are bought and sold by retail investors forever. He ultimately invents a new type of firm out of thin air—the discount brokerage house. It takes a few years before the Securities and Exchange Commission (SEC) even allows him to zag while the full-service guys are zigging. While the competitors of his brokerage firm are negotiating higher commissions, Schwab goes the other way, driving the cost of doing business with him to the bare minimum. He has set up shop in San Francisco and Sacramento, as far from Wall Street and its traditions as is geographically possible in the continental United States. He embraces technology to bring structure and efficiency to a very clubby and too-comfortable industry. Within five years, he is opening his twenty-third retail branch and offering 24-hour stock quotes to America's individual investors. Three years later, his firm opens its 500,000th customer account and sells itself to Bank of America for $57 million. By 1994, everyone in middle-class America is an investor, and the baby boomers begin coming into their peak earning (and investing) years. Charles Schwab & Company will hit $100 billion in customer assets under management that year and then over $1 trillion in 2002.

The American investor is now both blessed and cursed by an endless array of choices for how and with whom they want to invest. There are full-service brokerages, investment companies like mutual funds and hedge funds, asset managers, investment advisors, and discount brokerages. The amazing and ironic part of all that choice is in how similar all the marketing is for all the different options. The messages and images that all these different firms project are almost universally interchangeable.

3

Brokerage Oceanography

Before I continue, let me just draw one distinction that becomes more important as the story progresses . . .

When I use the term *brokerage firm* from here on out, I am primarily referring to the old-school broker-dealers, large and small, who make money from commissions and selling concessions that are charged to their brokerage customers on a transactional basis. Most industry participants have moved at least a portion of their business toward a more fee-based asset management or investment advisory approach, but there are still hundreds of thousands of products being pitched to retail brokerage customers every day, be they stock and bond trades, annuities, mutual funds, closed-end funds, underwritings, or unit investment trusts. We'll save our discussion of pure investment advisor firms for a later chapter.

~

You may have heard a thing or two about Wall Street's history on your own. The marketing stuff we've discussed will be familiar to anyone who's ever cracked open a magazine or watched a sporting event on television. What most people don't know much about, however, is how the modern-day brokerage firm works on the inside. The truth is that it really doesn't work at all. I didn't write this book to pick fights with the industry, but I've also not written it as a plain-vanilla, nonconfrontational Wikipedia entry. The regulatory rules as well as the desires of the customer base are diverging from the way that most brokers do business. This divide has been apparent and growing for some time now. Ultimately, this widening chasm threatens to swallow the brokerage industry's participants whole if they don't adapt. If the general public knew just how dysfunctional the modern brokerage firms have become over the years, there's a possibility that the entire enterprise would be flipped on its head and rewired from the ground up. This very idea is being pondered by Congress as I write. The sweeping Dodd-Frank financial reform bill that emanated from the 2008 crisis didn't leave the retail financial services sector completely out of its crosshairs, after all.

There is a metaphor that I use when both thinking about and explaining the way many brokerage firms operate these days. Do you remember reading those Richard Scarry children's books like *What Do People Do All Day*, the ones that were loaded with illustrations of cats, pigs, and birds living and working together in a rainbow-hued Small Town, USA? Well, you can look at the typical brokerage firm in much the same way, except that the archetypes we meet here are a bit more aquatic—sharks, whales, remora, jellyfish, and so on.

The sharks in my analogy are the revenue-producing registered representatives, more commonly referred to as the *brokers*. What's good for the brokers is good for the firm, and so they are essentially running the show. The brokers are the ones bringing in the clients, servicing their accounts, and generating the vast majority of sales for the firm—and they know it. Because the sharks are so aware of their importance, they throw their weight around, unlike the sales force in virtually any other industry. Managers and other personnel walk around the top-producing sharks as though they are on eggshells; a bookkeeper is replaceable, but a guy doing a million dollars a year in gross commissions isn't, at least not for the average branch office.

Support staff knows very well to stay out of the broker-shark's way because the sharks have a singular purpose each and every day: the selling of more product. As we all know, when a shark stops moving, it dies. When a broker stops selling, his or her practice dies; it's as simple as that. There's almost no such thing as "enough" when you are paid each fifteenth of the month for your gross commissions from the previous month. Each pay period is one-twelfth of the broker's annual income, and so each day within that period, somebody has to be closed on something. In New York's brokerage culture, this is called *buy or die.* I'm sure the Ed Jones boys in St. Louis had their own expression for it, as did the Raymond James folks of Florida. From Scottsdale to West Palm Beach to Boca Raton to the Hamptons, anywhere there were pockets of wealthy retirees, there were guys with 12 pay periods in which to get the job done. Those who work at the brokerage firm in a support role know better than to stand in the way of this; you'll rarely see the feeding frenzy interrupted by the sharks' fellow denizens of the deep. There is a simple math to how this works for the firm: more transactions good, fewer transactions bad. For the broker, this equation hits a bit closer to home: "Doing more transactions means that I keep my job. It also means that over time I add the assets of other brokers who are fired for doing too few transactions."

There are some qualitative calculations here in terms of which transactions pay better than others, but let's not get ahead of ourselves.

Suffice it to say, the sharks come in hungry each day, and they've got to eat, at least if they know what's good for them. Once they lose this hunger, they become susceptible to bigger, hungrier sharks coming along and chomping up their books of business.

When the shark has been a shark for long enough, he has accumulated some serious assets, assuming he hasn't been too aggressive headed into one of those hundred-year storms we seem to get in the stock market every seven years or so. With such a large and encumbering asset base, the transactions can slow; there is more than enough business to do without pushing as hard anymore. Fees are spilling out of every crevice and nook of that business, sloshing around onto the monthly pay runs in an effortless, almost inevitable manner. The shark has a touch of gray on the tips of his fins, and his teeth may be a bit worn down. But when the moment comes, well you just better believe he still knows how to bite. Yet, alas, his shark phase is now coming to a close. He will hence be treated and referred to as a whale: "That guy's been in the business since '85! He's a whale!" They're out there. Tough to recruit to other firms, they've already paid their dues and are quite comfortable with their current surroundings once they've gotten to this point. Their clients are too, and the secret to being a whale is maintaining as much stability for the clients as possible, regardless of business conditions. The inner monologue sounds something like this:

> So what if we were called DLJ last week and this week we are Credit Suisse? PaineWebber becomes Prudential becomes Wachovia becomes Wells Fargo becomes Burger King becomes *Merrill Morgan Joseph Smith Stewart Lynch and Sachs & Co.* So what? Who knows the difference anymore? The clients may have come in for the name of the firm, but they stay for the relationship with me! That

sense of constancy for the accounts, that ability I have to reassure them that somebody's paying attention and that there is one thing in their lives that will always be there. Who cares if I can get an extra 5 percent payout on my fees from the hotshot firm down the street? Everything is fine, I am happy, and my clients appreciate the continuity.

This is the whale's mentality at the brokerage firm. This is what the guy with 25 percent of the entire branch's assets under management thinks on his way to work each day; this is how he tolerates the jellyfish and the remora and the occasional toxic product dump into his territorial waters.

Of all the other fish in the sea with whom the whale must cohabitate, the most confounding relationship he has is with the dolphin—his *branch manager*. Branch managers and dolphins share several key traits, but the two most important are affability and a degree of intelligence. The branch manager must be friendly and playful, drinking beers with the brokers and keeping baseball tickets at the ready. But he (or she) must also be smart enough to know when it's time to commit the unthinkable—crossing the sharks and the whales. After all, it's the firm that pays the dolphin to maintain order. The branch manager is typically on a salary paid by the firm and has some upside based on the production goals of his branch. He is usually an ex-broker or a seasoned broker with a business that is manageable enough to allow him the extra time to supervise others—a "producing branch manager." He was the president of his fraternity and probably played on a ton of different teams growing up. He was only a middle-of-the-pack athlete but was able to earn the appreciation of the coach by helping stow the equipment away after practice.

The shelves in the office of our branch manager—let's call him Danny—contain the customary motivational books you expect to find from someone who refers to his brokers as "the troops." A volume of Sun-Tzu's *The Art of War* will be displayed prominently. You will see such airport motivational classics as *The Greatest Salesman in the World* and *Getting to Yes* and *The Millionaire Next Door* and *Think and Grow Rich!* and all the others, not one of them with even an ounce of stress showing on their bindings. They are coated with a fine film of dust—not surprising since the last time they were touched was when Danny got the promotion from assistant branch manager to branch manager three years ago and traded up to a slightly bigger office.

And it's a good thing that branch manager Danny is such an upbeat, friendly guy—because his job is impossible. I don't mean impossible in that it's undoable; people do this job every day all over the nation. I mean impossible in that it will not ever be done to the satisfaction of all parties. I became co–branch manager at my retail brokerage firm's New York City headquarters in December 2007, the all-time peak of the stock market. The timing of my promotion was almost cartoonish—like sauntering onto an X chalked on the sidewalk while a piano is hanging from a fraying cable 30 stories directly above. And as the Dow Jones dropped from 14,000 to 6,500 over the next 15 months, I came to realize that no matter what I did, no one would ever be truly happy with my performance, least of all me. I've instructed colleagues and friends of mine to hammer nails into my eyes if I ever mention that I'm considering a management role in a brokerage firm again. The branch manager position is a necessary but inherently futile one. In retrospect, I am lucky to have done it during the worst market downturn in 70 years; it sped up the process of my learning how much I hated doing that job. Though I may be smart and likable, I am very undolphin when push comes to shove.

Why is this role so completely illogical? There is a triangular tug-of-war for the branch manager's heart and soul each day, constantly threatening to tear the man or woman at the center to pieces.

The brokers tug at one end of the cord, "I want higher payouts, more expensed giveaways, more leeway on how I run my business, more leads, better assistants . . . and did I mention higher payouts?" As the branch manager, you are *one of the guys, on their side,* and *going to bat for your team* . . . until you can't. And then your team will grab the bat from your hands and jump you. Your top producer will De Niro–stomp you in front of the firm's owner. And that underdog guy you fought for when the firm wanted him fired? He will give you the dirtiest look of all when you ask him to do something as simple as move desks. It turns out that keeping hired-gun brokers in line and satisfied with their share of the treasure is not unlike the management of a pirate ship, and some of the most feared and respected pirate captains in history have fallen victim to a sudden mutiny.

In addition to the wants and needs of the brokers, there is another force exerting pressure; Danny's regional manager or firm owner wants to know why the branch isn't "more profitable, and also why isn't it growing? And what do you mean it can't get even more profitable at the same time as the branch grows, and why should we be writing so many checks for recruiting when the guys you recruited last quarter still haven't gotten all their assets moved over? And why aren't more of your guys using those new life-cycle funds we rolled out? And where are the referrals to the insurance group? You should see how much life and health biz Jack Mitchell's guys are doing down in the Charlotte office."

And as if there weren't pressure enough coming from both the brokers and the owners, here comes the compliance department, the jellyfish in my oceanic analogy. Here's what the branch manager hears when the branch's head of compliance approaches him, usually in the hallway en route to a meeting or appointment: "You can't seriously be signing off on this account, did you even see this guy's paperwork on it? I need you for five minutes when you get a chance, Danny.

And we have a new complaint I need you to look at from one of Alex's clients, I don't care how much of our monthly gross commissions come from his business, I don't like it. And then I need you for another two minutes to talk about this e-mail I saw go out this morning. And then can I see that file with our outgoing faxes from the last three months? And I need you for ten minutes after the close to talk about that other thing. And did you see this 'Notice to Members' from FINRA yesterday? We should probably have a meeting about that. I think it's important that you be there and not just have compliance explain it. Oh, and we also still need you for a moment before you head to lunch on that first thing I e-mailed you about this morning . . ."

It's a good thing branch managers are somewhat dolphinlike, because there is no shortage of hoops they need to jump through everyday.

We haven't heard much from the operations side of a typical brokerage firm yet. When we use the term *operations*, what we mean is the backbone of the entire firm, the people who move things from point A to B to C behind the scenes. If the operations people are doing their thing, a client should never see or hear of them; they are a coral reef suspending and sustaining an entire ecosystem beneath the surface.

There are compartments in the coral for paperwork and data to be processed and held in an accessible format. There are small pairs of eyes peaking out from the recesses of the coral's stolid presence, darting out and then inward before a passing broker has the chance to engage.

As a general rule, the last thing an operations person wants to get involved with is a personal issue with one of the salespeople—in fact, the attitude is very "keep those animals away from this room so we can do our jobs in peace." The brokers will notice errors or changes in various facets of their day-to-day business flow. They will come across prospective clients with nontraditional account registration needs. They will want to participate in certain offerings that are not facilitated with a simple point-and-click at their terminals. It is at these moments when the shark approaches the coral reef, and if words are not exchanged in just the right pleasantness of tone, there will be a skirmish. The funny part is, resolving these periodic battles between operations and the brokers means even more work for the already-beleaguered branch manager.

The sad part about these internecine struggles is that they won't matter. The broker-dealer in its current incarnation is dying anyway. According to the Financial Industry Regulatory Authority (FINRA), which polices brokers, there were 101 fewer broker-dealer firms at the end of 2010 from just a year earlier. The industry trade magazine *Investment News* estimates that the industry has dwindled down to only about 4,600 firms right now, having shrunk by 9 percent since 2005. The research firm The Compliance Department estimates that during the 12 months ended in May 2011, as many as 336 brokerage firms were shuttered. The firm foresees the ranks of the broker-dealer community shrinking by 11 percent, another 500 firms gone, over the next 3 years. Managing a brokerage firm in 2011 is a bit like shuffling the deck chairs on the *Titanic,* and anyone who says otherwise is utterly delusional.

A retail brokerage representative is the least sexy and most heavily scrutinized career one could have in the financial sector. The large firms like Merrill Lynch and Morgan Stanley simply gave up on recruiting new reps in large training programs like they did in the old days. Fortunately, the kids have demonstrated that they'd rather spend their first years out of college being unemployed than work in a wirehouse call center, anyway.

The very brokerage business model itself—selling products to investors based on a "suitability" standard—has been called into question. Many financial advisors have abandoned the traditional brokerage model, and those who still cling to it are now denying their obsolescence and waging an internal fight to the death that no one else seems to be aware of. Britain's main securities regulator, the FSA, has recently announced the end of commission-based financial services firms—in essence, no more retail brokerage. Don't fall out of your chair when the SEC ends up doing the same thing in the near-future.

But until that day, the sharks have to eat, and the whales need to eat even more. The jellyfish must sting to keep them all in line, and the dolphins need to keep everyone happy, even when there's little to be happy about.

When you look at a seemingly calm ocean, you can scarcely imagine the Darwinian doings beneath the waves. The cool, calm, and collected exterior of a brokerage firm in this day and age similarly obfuscates the strangling amount of tension just below the surface.

4

Of Brokers and Advisors

It's 4:30 in the afternoon on a sunny day in 1998. I'm at Gold's Gym in Garden City, New York, with the two senior brokers I am interning with for that summer, Steve and Greg. We work at a regional firm on Long Island, and every broker there leaves for the gym the minute the closing bell of trading rings. And they look it. I am a college kid surrounded by absolute Vikings who work hard and play harder. They are nonchalantly bench-pressing 315 pounds apiece while debating who has more gross commissions in for the day.

Greg looks up and stops talking midsentence and then whispers, "Stevie, you know who that is over there?"

"Shut up," says Steve, "it can't be! Is it?"

"Don't look at him, stop. He's coming over . . ."

Striding across the gym with one of those yellow Sony Walkman cassette players and a pair of weightlifting gloves is a guy who looks like he's famous even though I'd never seen him before. He's not tall, but not short either. His most notable feature is how perfectly coiffed his hair is, in the middle of a workout no less.

"What's up, fellas? You guys stockbrokers?" He can tell; it's something in the eyes or maybe the body language.

Greg speaks for us, "Yeah, we work over on Old Country Road. It's an honor to meet you. You need a spotter or whatever?"

The man my bosses are freaking out over is Al Palagonia. History knows him as the "Bucket Shop King," but in truth, he is one of the most talented retail stockbrokers who has ever wielded a telephone handset. In the early 1990s he worked at DH Blair, a now-infamous boiler room that specialized in pushing speculative IPOs like the world was coming to an end. Legend has it he took home a million dollars his first year in the business, and eventually he was making a million a month. Some say he had a shower and a bed installed in his office, so that when he was putting away shares of a hot deal, he'd never have to leave the phone. In a business characterized by aggression and avarice, he alternately scared the hell out of and inspired the other brokers to the point of oath-swearing. He worked so hard and made so much money for those around him that his guys would have lain in traffic on his say-so. When DH Blair was finally shut down by the regulators in 1997, Palagonia had his license stripped away and was barred from the securities industry.

It is about a year later, and Al is a legend in the eyes of all who know his story. Among retail brokers he is a god. We listen as he regales us with some of the most amazing stories we've ever heard. The sheer amount of stock he's put away and commissions he's booked is staggering. His friendship with Spike Lee is forged when Palagonia hooks the director up with his first courtside seats for the Knicks at Madison Square Garden. He will parlay that friendship into relationships with Michael Jordan and Shaquille O'Neal and speaking roles in a slew of Spike Lee films. If you've ever seen *He Got Game* (1998) with Denzel Washington and Ray Allen, the stockbroker-turned-actor played the sports agent with the driveway full of exotic cars.

As I head off to grab towels for the guys, I remember thinking, "Oh my god, this guy makes me want to break my neck to be successful!" I am as mesmerized by his story as I am by the way he tells it. And then I hear Al's parting advice to my star-struck senior brokers:

"You guys want my honest advice about the brokerage business?" They are hanging on every syllable. "Get the hell out." No one blinks, but Steve's jaw can be heard hitting the floor.

"Look, you seem like good guys. Believe me when I tell you, it's all over. There are much better ways to become millionaires in this world—so many opportunities to win, so many great businesses. No one's going to win the brokerage game, it's coming to an end. Find something else to do and just outwork everyone else, you'll thank me—I promise."

Al grabs his stuff and heads to the door, leaving the three of us trembling and confused. Greg and Steve don't mention the encounter to the other brokers back at the firm. I don't know where *they* are these days, but I know that Al Palagonia eventually got into the private plane business. He is now one of the leading jet brokers in the world, catering to athletes and celebrities and having the time of his life doing it.

He was right about the brokerage game; the end was near. We should've listened to him.

～

We certainly can't have a discussion about the sales tactics of Wall Street without first learning more about the various types of professionals who are actually doing the selling. The vast majority of contact between the investment industry and its individual clients is facilitated by two very different types of "professionals." The irony is that as different as they may be, the American public looks at them as though they are one and the same.

A lot of what I write in this book will be somewhat cathartic for me. As a retail broker, I spent a decade learning *what not to do.* During the summer of 2010, I dropped every single retail brokerage account I had and converted my practice away from transactions and toward the advice side of the business. Moving all my clients and making this transition almost killed me. The hundreds of thousands of forms, faxes, FedExes, e-mails, phone calls, and meetings to make it happen eventually landed me in the hospital—acute exhaustion coupled with the onset of a severe gastrointestinal attack.

It was well worth it, as I would soon realize.

By the time I was released from the hospital eight days later, a kind of euphoria overtook me. I was hit with a revelatory lightning bolt; it told me that everything had changed. After struggling to please the clients, the firm, and myself for 10 years and never succeeding at all three at once, the nightmare was finally over. I was now in a situation where my clients' success meant success for me and for my practice all at once—a virtuous and symbiotic relationship for all parties involved.

I remember walking through Penn Station on my first day back to work, bandages and bruises from the IVs still covering both arms, but with an irrepressible smile across my face. I was smiling so hard it was almost embarrassing; I didn't want the people bustling by me on the Long Island Railroad concourse to see my face lest they think me a crazy person. I hadn't felt so happy and so free ever before, professionally or personally. Even though I was faced with the challenge of beginning my career anew, I almost felt guilty at my good fortune at having left behind the very worst profession in all of financial services.

I will starve on the street before I will ever be a retail stockbroker again.

The strangest thing about stockbrokers is that no one on the outside truly understands what they do. As a quick introduction, stockbrokers get paid either a commission on the transactions they do for you (buying or selling stocks and bonds) or a selling concession paid to them based on products they sell to you (funds, IPOs, secondaries, banking deals, and private investments). They are only responsible to you on a trade-by-trade basis under the auspices of the *Suitability Standard*—meaning "Was the specific stock or fund or bond they sold you suitable based on your goals and risk tolerance?"

By contrast, investment advisors or financial advisors are paid for their ongoing advice in the form of a quarterly or annual fee. They are licensed with a Series 65 or 66 and overseen by some combination of the states in which they do business and the SEC. The firms they work for are known as registered investment advisors (RIAs), and the individual employees of these firms are called investment advisor representatives. They do not (and cannot) benefit by selling any specific product to you over another; their sole responsibility is to your financial well-being, and they must at all times act in your best interests. This nonconflicted relationship is conducted based on the *Fiduciary Standard*, a significantly more stringent requirement than the stockbroker's Suitability Standard, as it governs all aspects of the advice, not just advice that is incidental to a specific transaction.

Where things get tricky is when we're talking about what are known as dually-registered financial advisors, those who can act in the capacity of a broker when it suits them, earning commissions in some scenarios and advisory fees in others.

To illustrate the confusion that this type of arrangement can engender, here is an e-mail I received after a recent media appearance from someone whom I've never met or spoken with before.

Hi Josh,

Just signed on with a fiduciary (fee only advisor). By the third meeting, the only path that seemed to make sense was an annuity. I'm now very uncomfortable. How can he be a fee-only fiduciary and SELL me an annuity? He also, during what was a sales pitch, told me money going in, in the form of highly appreciated equities, could then be sold inside the annuity with no capital gains taxation to me. What do you think?

This kind of thing is very tough to avoid when clients don't fully understand the hybrid broker-advisor model and what it means in terms of the products and services they may end up getting.

I recently assisted a new client to make heads or tails of how and what he was being charged by his previous financial advisor for the last few years. Once we pieced together the trading confirmations and the quarterly statements, it turned out that he was paying a brokerage commission on every trade and a mutual fund load on each A-share purchase; and on top of that he was being charged a quarterly fee based on the entire account that annualized to 70 basis points (seven-tenths of a percent). The advisor-broker told my client that this was a "tactical fee." What a crock of sh*t. Basically my client had been paying brokerage commissions *and* an advisory fee on the same money.

I once was offered a position at a well-known and very successful independent brokerage firm that has pioneered the hybrid broker-advisor business model. I decided that no matter how much money in brokerage revenue I was leaving on the table, I just couldn't do that business for another second, hence my choice to go completely advice based. Most major firms offer employees some configuration of this dual business model and leave it up to the client to figure it out. You will very rarely overhear one of these hybrid broker-advisors explaining to a client that "on the sale of this mutual fund to you I am getting a concession from the fund family, but on the overall household accounts you've placed with me I am charging you 125 basis points for my role as your advisor." This is one of the dirtiest secrets in the business, and only the fractured community of purely independent advisors has an interest in shining a light on it. Exposing it is one of the best weapons a fee-only RIA rep has at his or her disposal when pitching new clients.

The astounding thing is that nobody has any idea that there even is a difference between stockbrokers and advisors. When I say "nobody," I mean *nobody*. Even some of the most sophisticated retail clients of brokerage firms often have trouble distinguishing between the two.

Consider these statistics from a September 2010 study by Infogroup/ORC:

- Two out of three U.S. investors (including 70 percent of 45- to 54-year-olds and 62 percent of college graduates) are incorrect in thinking that stockbrokers are held to a fiduciary duty.

- Some 76 percent of investors are wrong in believing that *financial advisors*—a term used by brokerage firms to describe their salespeople—are held to a fiduciary duty.

- By contrast, 75 percent of investors think the fiduciary standard is in place for financial planners, and 77 percent say the same about investment advisors.

- Over three out of five American investors mistakenly believe that stockbrokers are investment advisors.

There is discussion under way in both houses of Congress based on a recent SEC recommendation to study whether or not there ought to be two standards for financial professionals. My belief is that ultimately the brokerage standard toughens but does not approach the same seriousness as the advisors' fiduciary responsibility. It won't matter in the end; within a decade there will be more endangered giant pandas than retail brokers.

Investment advisors use this confusion to their advantage when chipping away at the client bases of the bulge bracket or wirehouse brokerage firms. Based on the *Charles Schwab Winter 2010 Independent Advisor Outlook Survey*, which polled 1,100 RIA participants managing $252 billion in assets:

> *Fully 86% of advisors surveyed say being independent gives them an edge over full-service brokerage advisors, while 83% say their role as a fiduciary helps them win new business.*

Other than those who've made the commitment to work conflict-free as independents, no one is making the effort to educate the public on what a broker does versus what an advisor does.

Before we move on, let me just say that having been a participant on The Street for a long time, I've known exceedingly honest and decent people on the brokerage side and hideously sleazy people on the investment advisory side. Even though I believe that one type of practitioner offers a far superior model for most investors, things are not exactly black and white. Advisors are in the headlines all the time for misappropriating client funds into their own personal deals and Ponzi schemes. In fact, the now-incarcerated Bernard Madoff ran a squeaky clean broker-dealer; it was on the investment advisory side (a de facto hedge fund) where his massive $50 billion fraud actually took place. There are good and bad actors in both camps; it's just that as a broker, you almost have no choice but to work against your customers in various instances.

If you have a stockbroker who consistently makes you money, then I suppose that congratulations are in order. You are quite literally one in a million, or one in ten million, perhaps.

I certainly don't mean to come off as holier-than-thou when discussing these differences. After all, it's not that stockbrokers are inherently bad people; I was a broker myself for a decade, and I still know some good guys in the business. No, the trouble with brokers is not necessarily a question of character or morality; rather it is one of architecture. The entire blueprint of the business is upside down. The compensation and incentives for brokers are set in diametric opposition to the best interests of the client. The interests of the firm fall somewhere in the middle of this curve, but closer to where the brokers are. It is sheer madness, and it has been status quo for a hundred years.

If you sat down with a team of economists, engineers, psychologists, and business ethics professors, you simply couldn't *create* a worse structure, no matter how hard you tried. It took me the better part of 10 years on the inside to figure this out, and I'm a pretty sharp guy. Now imagine how long it takes the average investor to figure it out—most never do.

Many of the honorable stockbrokers I know are only running the brokerage model at this point because they haven't yet seen the light or felt the urgency to evolve. I don't think the majority of them are truly fulfilled with their careers. They'll either make the change or become even more marginalized by lost-cost providers and regulators than they already are.

Until their eventual extinction.

5

Blue-Collar Wall Street

It is 8 o'clock in the morning on the North Shore of Long Island. The office is filled with rows of wooden desks; the walls are floor-to-ceiling tinted windows. There are no televisions in this room; there is only a giant whiteboard with motivational sayings scrawled across it. Below us, in the underground garage, Porsches and BMWs are taking naps as their owners (leasers?) are harangued upstairs.

The man standing before us is 300 pounds, and he is sweating profusely. He is Tony Soprano but bigger and more intimidating.

He has the type of bulky fat that you can tell was once muscle. He is so angry that veins are bulging from his hands, neck, and forehead. Maybe he is angry because of how he let himself go. He is acting as though he is angry at us, however, and we believe him.

We call him the "Mountain of Misinformation," but not to his face. He gives daily, hour-long meetings–slash–pep rallies that are completely divorced from reality; we are only taught what the firm wants us to learn. This is his fourth such meeting this week, his twelfth of the month so far. He could do 10,000 of these meetings without losing a drop of intensity. This is his gift.

He talks with his hands and takes periodic two-minute pauses in order to let his last sentence sink in. The pauses are more disconcerting than the words sometimes. He usually stands in front of the room but occasionally walks up and down the rows like a drill sergeant.

If you are smart, you avert your gaze lest it meet his. To look him in the eye will be interpreted as defiance, and defiance in a brokerage firm meeting like this one means death. It means "pack your stuff and get the hell out of here." It means that your clients and accounts will be handed to the other jackals right in front of you as you slink out the door, a samurai without a master, a broker without a book of business.

The Mountain has this power over us, and he knows it. He uses it to his advantage at all times. We don't have to think he's smart; obedience alone is enough for him.

"What is he even talking about?" I wonder to myself. I am just out of college and have no idea what this Mountain of Misinformation wants from my life. He is shouting at us at the top of his lungs about how we are blowing this opportunity to become rich. We owe it to ourselves, and apparently, we owe it to him. He warns us, something like, "Unless I see 10 new accounts opened before lunchtime, not a single one of you losers is leaving this boardroom for lunch." He is serious.

What am I doing here?

I am in my early twenties and too stupid to know that this wasn't what I wanted or signed up for. I am enduring abuse from a ruined, corpulent animal of a man whose IQ is probably half of what mine is, just as my waist size is half of his.

I look around me. Most of my fellow brokers are here because they didn't get the right education to really work on The Street. Some, like me, knew someone who told us to come in to this place and become big-shot successful brokers. But it's all wrong. This is not the white-collar world of financial executives and business lunches and client meetings and asset allocation. There is no 401(k), and there is no health insurance. Most of these people have no families and can pick up and disappear at the drop of a hat. They only pay their taxes when the IRS catches up with them. They are driving cars that will eventually be repossessed. They are overgrown children in Armani suits with maxed-out credit cards and very little knowledge of how money works. From 50 yards away, they look like financial professionals, but they are not. This is Blue-Collar Wall Street.

The yelling and screaming at the front of the room continues. This guy might seriously drop dead at some point; he is in a frenzy over our "not grasping the opportunity in front of us."

I already know I am leaving this backward place, where selling stocks is more important than recommending the right stocks . . . but not quite yet. There are some things I can learn here about work ethic. More importantly, these crazy sonofabitches can teach me how to close.

~

Have you ever received a cold call from a stockbroker? All these guys sound the same, right? That jocular introduction, the easy familiarity as they address you by your first name? This is all by design. "You better sound like you're in a good mood, or the guy on the other end will think you're not making people money! And call him by his first name, this establishes you as his equal. If you call him 'Mr. Jones,' he will never respect you."

The reason why every cold-calling stockbroker sounds the same is that this is a science, not an art form. There is a proven methodology that was developed in Lehman's Water Street and Madison Avenue offices in the 1970s and 1980s. It worked for 30 years. The returns on this type of cold calling began diminishing around the turn of this century, but there are some desperate brokers still at it. We'll get to them later.

Martin Shafiroff was one of the early practitioners of the cold-call stock sale. He literally wrote the book on it, called *Successful Telephone Selling in the '90s*. His success was later chronicled in a book called *The Winner's Circle*, which also featured one of the greatest stockbrokers of all time, the legendary Ace Greenberg of Bear Stearns. There was a legitimacy to what Schafiroff was doing, reaching out from Wall Street to share his knowledge with investors all over the nation. Shafiroff, in his mid-fifties by the 1980s, was operating a full-on sweatshop of cold calling out of the now-merged Shearson Lehman offices on Madison Avenue. People were shocked when a 1991 article in *Fortune* magazine first exposed this Street-wide practice:

> *Specimens of daily scorecards that the Madison Avenue office circulates to its cold-callers reveal a remarkable amount of activity. In the first four working days of October, 41 callers in one part of the office—including dialers, qualifiers, and brokers—got no fewer than 18,004 prospects to listen to at least a few words, qualified 1,208 of them, made 659 sales presentations to leads qualified on previous days, and opened 40 new accounts. A phone phenomenon was a $5-an-hour man named Steven Mitchell, who got through to 1,311 prospects in those four days, 98 of whom were subsequently qualified as leads. FORTUNE wanted to ask Mitchell about his work, but he said he was too busy to talk—and never called back.*

Shafiroff would remain at Lehman for decades, and by the mid-2000s he had built up the largest retail brokerage book in the country, $10 billion in assets under management. Marty eventually made it out and became an incredible financial advisor success story, but most of the guys who learned (and bastardized) his methods in the ensuing decades didn't.

As we were all told from the first day we picked up the phone to make our very first cold calls, Shafiroff started with nothing—no connections and no experience on The Street. After being rejected by several of the white-shoe firms of the era, he found his way to Lehman Brothers by 1969. He built his business over the telephone with corporate executives who had never met him in person. He was passionate about the value-oriented ideas he was pitching, and these ideas resonated with clients. With his educational background he could have been a money manager, banker, or analyst, but he chose to be a broker. In 2002 he explained why to *Registered Rep* magazine:

> *I decided to go into sales because I enjoyed communicating with people on a personal basis and felt I could apply my knowledge of securities in a more helpful and intimate manner.*

His telephone technique became known as the Lehman Method. In the late 1980s, if you had visited that Lehman branch, you'd have seen a big open boardroom with junior brokers dialing away in the center. All around them was a ring of glass offices. The difference between the losers in the middle and the winners surrounding them was that the guys in the offices were all standing up and pacing furiously as they pitched. They were hungrier and sold with a great deal more conviction—that's how they earned the offices to begin with.

That's how they kept those offices; if they slacked, it was back to the main boardroom. I know guys who were there. The markets were zooming, and the baby boomers were getting into stocks after a secular bear market that had lasted from 1966 until 1982. Cold calling was working.

This was the beginning of something that would be perverted and twisted into a great evil by the early 1990s.

Marty's original Lehman Method would spread and be learned far and wide. It worked. Ultimately, it would become known as the Straight Line Method because of its purposeful direction toward one end and one end only, the close. If you've ever been cold-called by a stockbroker, you've been treated to some variation of the Straight Line—I am 100 percent certain of this.

I want to emphasize here that we are not just talking about cold calling at small brokerage firms; the big wirehouses all had armies of cold callers too. If you were a broker at Merrill, Morgan, Smith Barney, Prudential, PaineWebber, Bear Stearns, Gruntal, or Oppenheimer, you spent at least half your days making dials back then. Not only was there no shame in it; your new account-generation and lead-obtaining skills were something to be proud of.

Eventually, the criminal element would get wise to this stock solicitation concept and its major financial possibilities. They would turn it into a way to pump sketchy stocks. The rise and fall of the notorious Stratton Oakmont and the other infamous boiler rooms had played out just as I was passing my Series 7. Many of the worst offenders had been or were about to be shut down. This was a blessing for investors but also a curse.

What happened next was unforeseeable to the regulators. The stockbrokers who survived the regulatory roundup simply kept the hyperefficient sales method they had learned but adapted it to more legitimate types of business—real stocks, real research, and decent deals to sell. The small firms were selling legitimate stocks to the public just like the big firms were, only with less compliance oversight and more leeway to abuse their customers. This adaptation prolonged a business that should have died at the end of the 1990s for an extra decade.

Sometime around the dot-com bust (2000–2002), the wirehouses and super-regional firms began to adapt their business model and retrain their employees. The registered reps would augment their Series 7 credentials with Series 65 and 66 licenses, which enabled them to become financial advisors, not just brokers. This would cut down on customer complaints and make client money "stickier" than traditional brokerage accounts. The reps would get their Life and Health licenses so that they could also sell insurance policies and annuities. This was occurring just as the firms they worked for were basking in the glow of Glass-Steagall's repeal. The brokerages were merging with banks, and the reps were now working at "financial supermarkets."

By 2005, wirehouse brokers were calling themselves *financial advisors* exclusively. By 2007, they were beginning to refer to themselves as *wealth managers*. By 2008, they would, as a group, preside over a bonfire of that wealth they were supposed to have been managing—but that's a story you've probably heard (or witnessed) already.

The wirehouse's disuse of the term *stockbroker* has not stopped a last, lost tribe from carrying on the cold-calling tradition into the 2010s. There are still a handful of broker-dealers left that sell stocks and private placements over the phone using the Straight Line Pitch or some derivation thereof. They are a dying breed, though the few successful ones don't seem to know it.

The last brokers standing have survived a decade of blowing up their clients and having to repeatedly get new ones. They have weathered the mass proliferation of the online brokerages, which do what full-service brokerages offer for a fraction *of a fraction* of the cost. They have endured as the NASD, now FINRA, made rule after rule about churning, excessive commissions, and suitability, the three worst enemies of a broker trying to "do big gross."

Will they survive another 10 years of smarter investors, regulatory scrutiny, and online discount rivals? It is doubtful. Even their own self-regulatory organization (SRO) wants to see the small broker-dealers disappear. There are a disproportionate amount of customer complaints against these firms, and the regulators know that the firms offer nothing of value to their customers. Many of the firms that have facilitated this brand of churning over the years have been shut down either because of investigations and charges or because they've simply run out of money. It is hard to stay in business when you need to replace half of your customers every year and a big chunk of your top producers are fined and prosecuted out of the industry.

But a few brokerages are still out there doing things the old-school way. Ironically, these quasi-boiler rooms are the only firms that are still actually on Wall Street itself. All the major firms have relocated either to the west side (World Financial Center) of Manhattan or to Midtown (known as Wall Street North). The "kids in suits" are still down on Wall Street or Broad Street because, like their slick appearance and gaudy watches, they think their proximity to the Stock Exchange lends them an air of authenticity. If a broker tells you he works on Wall Street, run.

When you walk into these firms, to a certain extent you are walking through a museum—a living exhibit of how things used to be in the brokerage business. There are still young men (very few women are around other than sales assistants and receptionists) cajoling their customers in urgent tones over the phone to "make a move before it's too late." The trainees are still learning to cold-call for the all-important leads. Their senior brokers still close those leads while delivering the Straight Line Pitch, just as it has been done since before the Internet or cell phones or the war on terror. The young recruits still rhapsodize about "getting their Seven," as if it's some kind of serious professional designation or a license to print money. They are still buying leads to call in rural areas, where "the guys are too polite to hang up on you" or "they love hearing someone from New York tell them about a hot stock." They are still guzzling Red Bull energy drinks, listening to every word at those brutal morning meetings, and learning nothing about the markets or portfolio management; they are only taught how to sell and sell hard.

> *"Buy or die." "Get back on the phones." "Never mind what the market is doing, dial that phone." "What do you mean research? Your script is the only thing you need to know."*

Poor kids. Many of them just wanted to work on Wall Street. They thought that's what they were learning to do. But they are not engaged in any kind of money management; nothing they do is helpful to anyone. They are wasting their time, and many of these kids don't realize it until it's too late. One mark on your license, and you can kiss the legitimate training programs goodbye; you're done.

When people ask me about my time spent on Blue-Collar Wall Street, I tell them the truth. I tell them that I learned exactly what *not* to do. Every day I see others make mistakes with their investments that are obvious to me. I have been galvanized and tempered in a way that almost none of my colleagues can imagine.

I am stronger and wiser than many of them as a result.

6

Mamas Don't Let Your Babies Grow Up to Be Brokers

"Alright guys," said the freckled, boyishly chubby sales manager in the front of the boardroom. "The pay period ends at the close of business today. One more chance to put together a decent f*ckin' month, one last chance to get some gross in for your check on the fifteenth."

All eyes on him. You can hear the old time-stamping clock we used for trade tickets clicking away in the background, and that's about it.

"So what's it gonna be? You guys gonna be brokers or a bunch of f*cking pikers?"

This guy's not nearly as intimidating as the Mountain of Misinformation was. He's younger and weaker, and he's made the cardinal mistake of going out drinking with the young guys on a regular basis. Once your brokers see you get grinded on by a stripper or watch you fall all over yourself at a happy hour, you're pretty much done.

But this guy didn't understand that. He thought access was his strength, the access that any of the brokers had to him, from the biggest producers to the smallest cold callers. Everybody's buddy, the big-shot broker you could go to for anything. And he reveled in the adulation. That was his drug. We may not have feared him, but we respected him, and he was intoxicated by it. The brokers, predominantly male and in our early twenties, respected that he was driving a Benz two-door convertible. We also respected that every month—every pay period, I should say—he found a way to get over six figures in business done. He always found gross commissions to do no matter what.

"Now a lot of you are looking at me like I don't understand," he continued. "Like I don't know what it's like to be in down stocks and have clients to answer to." He is pacing now, all *blue shirt and white collar and yellow tie and spiked hair.* "But believe me when I tell you, I have more down stocks and pissed-off clients than anyone in this room. And I guarantee you that by the close of business today, I'll have another 15 in gross done to finish out the month."

He definitely will, we all nod.

"And you know why? You know what the difference is between me and everyone else? I want it. I need it. I'm hungrier than everyone here, which is a f*cking embarrassment considering I already make more than every single person in this boardroom." It's not true, but the big producers who would normally object don't have to sit through harangues like this; they are in their offices while their apprentice brokers (like me) are being lectured by Big Shot.

"Jimmy," he shouts at a midlevel guy without even turning around to face us, "what business are we in?"

Jimmy replies as if by rote, "We're in the moving business."

Big Shot's first syllable steps on the hem of Jimmy's last: "Hear that, boys? We're in the *moving* business, we ain't in the *storage* business.

You got a position not working out, today is when you sell it and you do that *G*. You write those tickets today no matter what, I don't give a f*ck what story you need to tell."

He pauses for emphasis, just like all those ugly sales books he's read have taught him to do. "Now some of you guys are still looking at me like I don't get it. Like I don't understand how hard you pushed these positions on your clients and how great you've told them these stocks are. Ya know what? Too bad. *You're* the broker, *you're* calling the shots. The clients are paying you for your expertise, and you need to get that across on all your calls today, period."

Audible gulps can be heard in the boardroom as the gears are turning and the *kids in suits* are already concocting excuses for why their clients need to make a commission-generating move today.

"This isn't about what your client thinks, this is about what y*ou say*. The minute the client is dictating which stocks he holds and which stocks he sells, you *lose*. You've lost control of the relationship, and you might as well rip his posting page out of your book, it's over, fellas."

Today is going to suck. People are going to do things that their consciences tell them not to do as a sacrifice to the God of the April Pay Period. Lines will be crossed, bullsh*t will be spewed, and trades will be done that have absolutely no justification other than some broker's overdue car payment.

"So listen up, guys. Go down and grab your coffees and smoke your butts and whatever else you need to do, 'cause when that opening bell rings, I want every one of you on the phones, smiling and dialing. And as an added incentive—and this is coming from the partners—the bottom producer this month is fired. The top three producers get his book of clients. Do yourself a favor and don't be that loser who has to pack his sh*t and leave. Get on the phone and get some G done no matter what. Rock n' roll."

There is applause at the end of the meeting; no one dares to be caught not clapping it up with the rest of the monkeys. Papers are shuffled, Quotrons are booted up, and a half-dozen brokers head for the elevators to chain-smoke two or three cigarettes so they can make it through the morning. Maria Bartiromo is defending her personal space on the floor of the NYSE on TV screens around the football field–sized boardroom. The first handful of outbound calls can be heard as a few frightened rookies skip the chance to grab coffee and get right down to business.

And before long, you can hear phone receivers slammed down and see paper tickets flying into the trading room. High fives are exchanged, and guys who score big orders are writing the details on a massive dry erase board at the front of the room for all to see— part motivation, part shaming of the guys who haven't gotten the job done yet.

The young men so diligently working to please Big Shot all have families at home. Moms and dads and grandparents and girlfriends who think that their precious David or Billy is a stock market professional. Instead, the prodigal son is pounding the phones out of a misplaced fear of failure, ruining his future career prospects in the process. He will be accumulating marks on his license and learning nothing useful about the market, all in the service of the pay-period grindstone he is chained to. He will be alienating every client he manages to talk into giving him a shot, hence the constant need to open new accounts and bring in new money. The *old* money's been traded away or blown up in an unfortunately concentrated bet.

Oh well, get back on the phones.

Just so you know, the picture I've painted is straight out of the late 1990s, but you can still find this type of thing happening today. It is usually taking place in New Jersey, on Long Island, or down on Wall Street now that all the big firms have moved uptown. Only the brokers that need the validation and patina of prestige that comes from having a Wall Street address are actually still located there.

The thing you need to know about the brokers who call you up out of the blue is that they are essentially telling you casual lie after casual lie until even they have forgotten what's real. The kid who calls you up and reminds you that "the last stock I brought to you was Netflix six months and 100 points ago" has repeated this falsehood on so many calls that by the time he gets you on the phone, he is almost convinced that he did. Listen to the conviction and the sincerity in his voice! It must be true! "OK, kid, I'll play along. Whaddya got today?"

Large firms like Smith Barney and Merrill Lynch did so much cold calling and pitching over the phone that they literally got too big to do any more. They now have so many accounts that they've opened call centers to handle the overflow of clients.

A recent review on the employment site GlassDoor.com said this about working at a Merrill Lynch "call-center sweatshop":

> *You will get burnt out after 6 to 12 months, the turnover is extremely high because people quickly realize they are being overworked, Long Hours, Unpaid Overtime, No real room for advancement, Constant change of goals which makes it hard to really determine how much you will make. Advice to Senior Management: Morale is low because you constantly change the goals and you are never satisfied. You know people are unsatisfied which is why you are constantly running new hire training classes every 3 months.*

Merrill Lynch has rebranded its call centers under the Merrill Edge moniker. Like most wirehouse firms, Merrill has been moving its full-service brokerage operations "upstream." It only allows those with $100,000 in assets or more to be assigned to a dedicated registered rep, and it considers the $250,000 account size and up its "sweet spot." Any accounts smaller are handed off to the Merrill Edge steerage-class section. This philosophy of managing fewer accounts but of larger size is being adopted by brokerages all over the country; even the notoriously folksy regional player Edward Jones has announced an initiative of this sort.

These days, because the larger firms now have so many clients that they need to build call centers just to service them, cold calling has taken a backseat to client development (money raising from existing accounts) among the established players.

But, yes, the cold-calling small brokerage firms still exist even if they are dropping like flies. I got a postcard mailed to my house two years ago that literally scared the children. It featured the bald-headed, rabid-looking "CEO" of one of these firms pointing at me with the demand that I come down and "learn to be a million-dollar producer." Maybe some other time, freak.

There's another firm downtown with a football stadium–sized scoreboard that displays everybody's gross commissions for the day in the middle of the office. How wonderful for the clients; I'm sure they'd be thrilled. No worries; most of them live thousands of miles away and will never have the privilege to see it.

There's also a firm where the brokers' chairs are taken away if they're seen to be slacking or not "pitching hard enough" on the phone. I'm told by guys who've worked there that the doors are locked at lunchtime if there aren't enough new accounts opened by noon each day. You'll notice that these guys say the word *accounts* as opposed to *clients*. This dehumanizing makes it easier for the reps to churn them and treat the money as fodder for commissions. This is a military tactic that generals have used for a thousand years to desensitize the troops to the fact they were killing other human beings. It's much easier to pull the trigger when facing "the Skinnies" or "the Gooks" or "the Towelheads" or "the Japs" rather than actual people.

One firm has its own Red Bull vending machine in the office so that its *Jersey Shore*-esque hired guns can keep themselves "pumped" all day. You'll know the building by the cloud of cigarette smoke in front of it and all the guys in three-piece pinstriped suits crowded around the front. And if you walk by at the right time of day and meet the right broker standing there, you might even be offered your Series 7 books right on the spot—"Come up and pound the phones with us, buddy! We'll train you to be a million-dollar producer!" Anyone who is willing to casually lie about his or her ability to outperform the markets can work there. You will not be asked about your education or background, only whether or not you have any felonies so the company doesn't waste its time trying to license you. *Old school* does not even begin to describe the mentality.

Very few of these brokerages are left, now that paying 3 percent commissions is laughable to all but the most clueless investors. What low commissions couldn't kill, the regulators have maimed; many cold-calling firms like Joseph Stevens and Gunn Allen have been fined out of existence for everything from aggressive sales practices to net capitalization violations. Shutting down a notorious boiler room for a technical accounting breach is a bit like putting Capone in Alcatraz for tax evasion, but the end result is the same. The few of these types of firms that still live have simply become the concentrated repository for all the brokers with nowhere left to go. They've gotten insanely good at playing the compliance game, doing and documenting everything to the letter of the law while pushing the envelope to the very edge. They have found that gap between illegality and amorality, and they are exploiting that gap on a daily basis. They own that gap and cannot be dislodged from it until the rules change. And then they'll simply adapt again.

But just because you *can* do something, it doesn't mean that you *should*. There are those in the brokerage business that will never comprehend this.

I used to look at my time among the brokers as time wasted, but now I know the truth. It turns out that my exposure to brokerage culture is a major asset to me now as I manage portfolios and investments. This is because I've received a crash course in reckless market behavior. For years I had front-row seats for the Olympic Games of investing stupidity. Without even realizing my good fortune, it turns out that I had learned exactly what *not* to do at a very young age, and I've made very good use of that knowledge ever since.

7

How I Learned to
Close Anyone

I have a particular skill, honed over the course of 15 years, that should make you very afraid . . . except for the fact that I don't use it anymore.

I can close anyone. And I do mean *anyone.*

Given the names and phone numbers of three qualified (wealthy) investors, I could turn one of them into a stock-purchasing client within one phone call, guaranteed.

When I explain this to civilians who have never worked in (or near) the brokerage business, they are in disbelief that such a thing could even be possible. They have no idea.

Having been schooled intensively in the art of the Straight Line Pitch, as created by Lehman and other firms of that era, I had evolved the technique over the years to a precision-guided state of utter perfection. With only my pitch and the manner in which

I delivered it, I had spurred the writing of tens of millions in checks and the buying of hundreds of different stocks by thousands of different people from all over the United States, Canada, the United Kingdom, Australia, and New Zealand. I worked from 8 a.m. to 7 p.m. five days a week and at least one day on the weekends during my first three years in the business. I had become well versed in every single type of rejection you could think of and several that I cannot print here for the sake of good taste. Not only had I become conditioned to expect these various types of rejections; I had been trained to welcome them, to salivate for them so that I could put each objection to bed until there was nothing left for the prospect to say but yes.

I had made the Straight Line my own over time, removing excesses and adding personal flourishes that allowed me sell stock over the phone morning, noon, and night, Monday through Sunday. I had become fearless and unstoppable, lethal with a telephone and a hot investment idea.

I'm not proud of all the skills I learned during that period of my life. It was my job. I was too young when I began and had followed some of the wrong types of role models in my early, developmental years. This time spent on the wrong track would ultimately turn out to have been a blessing in disguise, but it took me a long time to realize that.

By the age of 19, after my freshman year at the University of Maryland, I had become a pretty good cold caller. I learned to get 30 working-age millionaires on the phone at their places of business and have 10 of them answer my qualification questions (the names of stocks they owned, the brokerage firms they were working with, a dollar-amount estimate of their total portfolio, a ballpark figure they would normally put into a new stock recommendation, etc.). These were my leads for the day, and if I didn't have them to hand in to my senior broker by the close of business, my summer position at the firm was over. And it was not just the amount of leads I generated that I was judged on. We kept dial sheets, and we were judged on the amount of times we were hung up on. The more hang-ups the better, as counterintuitive as that may sound. Getting clicked meant you were hustling; it meant you were getting enough nos to reach the next yes and the yes after that.

Five days a week that grueling summer I showed up at an office building on Third Avenue in Manhattan at 7 a.m. and sat down on the floor of the hallway waiting for the office doors to be unlocked. There would be a few dozen of us waiting there each morning because there were 100 cold callers and only 75 desks. This meant that each day 25 people were sent home before the brokers they worked for had even arrived. If you were sent home three times, you were fired and replaced within an hour; there were hundreds of applicants for every desk in that room back in 1996. It was the very peak of the Age of the Stockbroker, and I was a wide-eyed kid just trying to hang onto my slot until the fall.

Upon beginning my first full-time job at a brokerage firm a few years later, it occurred to me that the only things I had been taught up until that point were related to sales as opposed to the markets and investing. "Shut up and dial the phone" was the response I received when I raised this issue with a senior guy at the firm. Looking back, I'm amazed I didn't crawl back home and beg my parents to send me to law school right then and there, but I had just passed my Series 7 and was way too enthusiastic to turn away from the business just then.

Before I forget, let me just address this Series 7 business right here so we can get it over with. The Series 7 is the primary license that stockbrokers (called *registered representatives* in the regulatory vernacular) must attain to begin selling securities to the public. It is a 250-question exam that teaches the young and aspiring broker absolutely nothing of any utilitarian value. There is virtually zero knowledge that the broker takes from this test and puts to good use once his or her career begins. All the calculations we learn for the exam are done with computers in the real world. The sections of the test on ethics are obvious to the point of stupidity. All the securities laws you learn about date back to the 1930s and are totally irrelevant in the context of the abuses that are so prevalent today. The test itself is merely a six-hour barrier of entry so that not anyone off the street can sell securities. And as far as barriers go, it is a weak one; I've known people who could not tie their own shoes who have passed the test over the years.

Upon passing the test, the cold caller or "connector" earns a new title: account opener. This is where the tactics and "resistance to resistance" that I had learned began to pay the bills. The account opener's job is to take the qualified leads and turn them into actual client accounts. "Hi Bob, last week you had spoken with a member of my staff about my firm Harrington & Company, we sent out some literature which I hope you've enjoyed with my compliments. Today we have isolated one of the most undervalued stocks on the entire exchange. If you'd like to take some notes, I'd be glad to share it with you." Just typing those words makes me want to vomit into a waste-basket, but for better or for worse, I've delivered an introduction like that more than 100,000 times.

Traditionally, brokers at wirehouse firms like Paine Webber and Merrill Lynch were working on teams. The account opener was typi-cally a guy in his mid-twenties who had paid his dues cold-calling for the team and serving in a sales assistant–phone answering capacity until such time as the senior brokers felt that he was ready to pitch stock (or bonds or funds). At that point, the account opener (or junior broker) would be responsible for bringing in anywhere from 20 to 50 new accounts with minimum opening sizes of $5,000 to

$25,000, depending on the firm. The account opener was not to open any new clients with less than $250,000 in household liquid assets. At the larger firms, those minimums ultimately trended higher; most clients of Merrill Lynch with less than $250,000 in their Merrill accounts are now handed off to centralized call centers as opposed to having traditional brokers assigned to them.

At the other end of the spectrum, minimum account sizes at the smaller firms have trended lower as the less robust offerings of the under-siege small brokerages led to a "take whatever you can get" culture. It is not uncommon to see small-firm brokers fight over $7,000 IRA accounts these days as a 2.5 percent commission on flipping that principle five times a year can add up to a few hundred dollars in gross commissions each quarter.

The dedicated and ambitious account opener immerses himself in the ways of the Straight Line. It is his religion. By this time, he has spent months cold-calling during the day and studying for his exams at night. He is starving, both financially and emotionally, for a taste of success. This is fortunate, because only the very hungriest will be able to surmount the next obstacle with their mental state intact.

The account opener studies the rebuttals to various objections before he goes to sleep each night; he memorizes the different closes over the sandwich he brought from home at lunchtime. Without his rebuttals and closes, he will not bring in the requisite accounts to reach his objective and will likely be fired. He cannot afford to ever be at a loss for words or to run out of ammunition on the phone, regardless of what he's pitching. There were only three objections that were ever "real" according to the methodology:

1. A recent death in the family

2. A bankruptcy

3. An ongoing divorce

Only in those three cases were we trained to move on. In two of the cases, there are frozen assets; in the other, well, we were not monsters after all (at least most of us weren't). Any other objection besides those meant that we just hadn't found the client's buying points yet. This meant we should keep the discussion going, keep pitching. Eventually, the client would either hang up or authorize a trade, sometimes just to shut you up, other times because he had been won over and convinced that the investment was in his best interest.

As a quick aside, you'll notice that I'm using the masculine pronouns *he* and *his* and *him* while I dissect the process of account opening and pitching stock. This is not accidental. I would estimate that more than 90 percent of the brokers who had come up this way in the business were male and that 99 percent of the affluent investors on the other end of the phone have been male as well. This is by design, as the pitch and progression from lead to account to client are all very much built around appealing to the male psyche. It is nearly impossible to impulse-sell securities to women, as they tend to invest more for financial security than for bragging rights, big fish tales, or naked greed like wealthy men do.

I'm not interested in turning this discussion into a battle of the sexes; it is a fact that men (including myself) have deep-seated insecurities about money and about missing out on the opportunity to make more. Over decades the Straight Line Pitch and variants of it have succeeded in exploiting these insecurities, but it just didn't seem to elicit the same kind of response from members of the fairer sex. Because this was the case, most efforts to pitch women over the phone were abandoned early on and never attempted again. The irony here is that this institutionalized bias ensured that those brokers were never actually talking to the *real* decision maker in the family. There was always this stigma to "talking to the wife" in the old days. When counseling rookie advisors and less experienced industry participants, one of the first myths I shatter for them is this one. These days, some of my best and most satisfying client relationships are with the female heads of the households I serve.

But I digress . . .

Upon the opening of his final owed account, the junior broker now faces the choice of remaining with his team (though for a larger share in the business) or going on his own. Either way, he is no longer just an account opener or a junior broker; he is now given the right to carry on relationships with clients, despite the fact that he must still spend the lion's share of his day drumming up enough new accounts for himself in order to survive.

It is at this point that the very worst of the financial services industry manifests itself and lays heavy over the investment landscape. For it is at this point that a professionally trained salesman is empowered to begin making investment decisions for and with the general public. Having spent every waking hour learning to sell with only the bare minimum of market knowledge attained in order to do so, the registered rep is now making recommendations to investors on an ongoing basis. This is the scene in the action movie where the car goes off the cliff, the Shakespearean denouement during which irreversible tragedy befalls the well-meaning protagonist and his best-laid plans.

Most of the brokers I know and have met over the years are phenomenal, world-class salespeople. Like me, they have learned an ironclad sales rap that, when employed prodigiously and often, produces a logic-defying amount of income. But a great many of these securities-selling savants don't attain the knowledge necessary to actually accomplish anything for their clients. As I have come to learn over the years, selling one's expertise is much easier than actually developing an expertise, especially as it pertains to investing.

Let me not dance around this simple and ineluctable truth a moment longer: brokers have no business making investment decisions for anyone.

In Bob Dylan's song "Knockin' on Heaven's Door," the folk rocker plaintively suggests that his guns should be taken from him as they are no longer of any use. Having hung up my retail brokerage badge and holsters myself, I certainly can relate to the sheriff character Dylan embodies in that remorseful western dirge.

I can say without even a tinge of regret that my ability to rapid-fire close people has probably begun to leave me by now. While I still work in the securities business, I now sit on the same side of the table as the client. There is no need or benefit to sell products anymore, and so that part of my professional repertoire is now vestigial, still with me but not in use. It was something learned, and as with all acquired talent, it can just as easily become something forgotten. I certainly wasn't born with the talent to sell; in fact this talent was quite hard-earned, as it goes against my very nature and personality.

Suffice it to say that my only consolation for those years is that I attempted to use my abilities for good at every turn. To this day I can proudly claim to have never received a single complaint from any customer or compliance officer for as long as I had been in the brokerage business, a point of pride for me given the nature of it all. I never took any shortcuts with the truth and never used these persuasive powers of mine for evil. This is probably one of the reasons why I ended up having to leave the brokerage industry entirely in the end—I simply wasn't cut out for it.

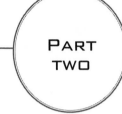

PART
TWO

THE PRODUCT

We now have an equity fund industry that's worth $2 trillion,
and if everyone wants their $2 trillion back
tomorrow, they're not going to get it.
—John Bogle

The only logical reason to play the game of active
investing is that you place a high
entertainment value on the effort.
—Larry Swedroe

When you realize that you are riding a dead horse,
the best strategy is to dismount.
—Sioux Indian proverb

8

Brokerage Goes Digital

Now that we've established that retail brokers are the devil, let's look at the self-directed alternative. There's been an awful lot of money and time spent to convince the teeming investor masses that they are better off going it alone. In some cases this may be the truth. So what are their options?

Fortunately for the self-determined, they have a nearly unlimited array of choices in how they can run their own show. The original revolution sparked by Charles Schwab in the late 1970s and early 1980s really flourished in the digital era, as costs came down and capabilities blossomed. Just as the Internet revolutionized retail shopping, dating, publishing, and the business of getting information, so too did it facilitate a new paradigm of investing. It also played havoc with everyone's margins—more on that in a bit.

The traditional discount brokerages found a whole new cadre of investors on the Internet in the late 1990s. Formerly staid firms like Brown & Company, Olde, National Discount Brokerage, and Waterhouse remade themselves in their new online environs and dragged their existing customers with them for the ride.

Upstarts like DLJ Direct, Datek, E*TRADE, and Ameritrade were not necessarily taking business from traditional discount brokers at the outset; they were merely helping the vertical itself find a higher level of respectability among the investor class. No longer were "relationships" a deciding factor in terms of who would be successful and who would be merely a misguided investor left by the wayside. All of a sudden it was hip to be making one's own decisions about which stocks to buy.

By the beginning of 1998, it became apparent not only that online brokerage was here to stay, but that it would now be a powerful force within the investing industry on an ongoing basis. In the first quarter of 1998, the overall volume of all securities traded over the Internet was up 25.5 percent from the fourth quarter of 1997. There were 192,000 online trades made in the first three months of that year versus 153,000 in the prior three-month period. Schwab's customers' online trades made up 31 percent of this volume, while customers' transactions at E*TRADE were 12 percent.

This was not just a new segment within the brokerage business; it was a revolution. What came along with this rapid adoption and scale were significantly lower commissions, as everyone joined the landgrab for new customer accounts. It was a scorched-earth affair, to be sure; the average commission charged by the top 10 online brokerages plummeted 54 percent throughout 1997, from $34.65 to $15.95 per trade.

And of course, the early adopters of online trading were primarily interested in buying the stocks of other online companies.

Internet companies were the trading and investing vehicles of choice for the first online players, which worked out well, as this era coincided with the biggest tech stock frenzy in history. It wasn't just ethically compromised analysts like Henry Blodget or Mary Meeker that propelled Internet stocks to unspeakable valuations in those early days of online stock trading; they had a very willing accomplice in the army of E*TRADERs who had completely bought into the new "paradigm-shift" argument and the exhortations from so-called experts that "this time it's different."

They were egged on by the marketing machinery of the online brokerages themselves. In retrospect, the advertising fanfare of this period represented the absolute pinnacle of irresponsible Wall Street marketing—worse than anything being perpetrated by the traditional brokerage firms at that time. Actually, it was borderline psychotic.

The central conceit of the online brokerages' ad campaigns back then was that any schmuck could be a billionaire and that riches were only clicks away. This was the financial services equivalent of Atlantic City casinos busing in senior citizens to pump the last of their social security money into slot machines. So audacious were the marketing efforts of that era that even now, more than a decade later, we haven't seen anything even remotely as wild.

I have a YouTube collection of commercials I've saved from that era. I post them on my Web site from time to time to remind myself and others not to allow the media to whip us into a speculative frenzy. Allow me to remind you of some of the more egregious examples of the frenzy to illustrate my point.

The one that most of us remember involved a tow truck driver with a postcard of paradise rubber-banded to his sun visor. When asked about the photo, he nonchalantly tells his passenger that it is not just any island; it is actually *his* island. Bought and paid for with the profits from his online trading. Seriously.

There were also several shockingly embarrassing examples from that era that involved sports figures like Shaquille O'Neal and Anna Kournikova dispensing investment tips and using terms like PE ratio to great comedic effect. Like it was all a big, riotous joke, and only a loser wasn't minting money right now. Anna in her tennis whites, taking the time between not winning any majors and being photographed in compromising states of undress, making us feel foolish for not kicking ass in the stock market. It was all so easy, after all—just open a brokerage account and commence being rich.

Famed Chicago Bulls coach Phil Jackson had an online brokerage commercial as well. In the back of a limousine he mentions that he is about to make a major trade. The chauffeur leans back in order to hear it, expecting it may involve the fate of his favorite NBA team. Turns out, Coach Phil is referring to a big trade for his online brokerage account—ha-ha-ha! Look how casual and fun investing is; throw another retirement log onto the fire, Joe Sixpack!

Of all the shockingly irresponsible commercials, however, one reigns absolutely supreme in terms of its sheer idiotic conception and execution. Of all the chimpanzees in diapers and celebrity Buffett-wannabes, nothing else even comes close to this level of immaturity and insult. The spot I'm referring to involves kung fu superstar Jackie Chan fighting off a gaggle of evil henchmen while placing a trade with TD Waterhouse. Jackie battles these black-clad ninjas while researching a stock on a laptop in his living room. Apparently he's concluded his intensive due diligence on this particular stock investment because while running horizontally across the walls and sparring with these martial arts marauders, he feels no compunction about tossing the laptop over his head, throwing a punch to the face of an assailant, and then leaping into the air to kick the buy trade into the keyboard with his karate master toe.

Nothing up until this moment (or since) had so thoroughly disrespected what it means to be an investor in the stock market. These commercials represented the peak of do-it-yourself madness, the alpha and the omega of insolence toward the investing profession. The fact that the NASDAQ itself would subsequently drop by some 80 percent shortly thereafter was a well-deserved punishment for just this sort of charlatanism. While E*TRADE and Ameritrade survived, many of the smaller online brokerage firms disappeared into mergers with their larger competitors once stock trading ceased to be the national pastime.

Perhaps the best coda to that mania I could offer here would be to tell you what the commercials looked like a year after the market's 2000 crash. In the wake of such an epic bust for a majority of investors and traders, the last thing the online brokers wanted was to share any of the guilt. No, the mania wasn't at all their fault, and to prove it, the dopey celebrities and billionaire truck drivers were replaced with grown-ups. TD Waterhouse will trot out the curmudgeonly Sam Waterston, ripped straight from the set of *Law & Order* on which he played a conscientious and reliable prosecutor for so many years. Old people love him, and young people respect him; he's the perfect guy to cover the carnival barkers' retreat and to instill a little gravitas into the equation. Almost overnight, the circus atmosphere becomes a dignified funeral, Waterston in a drab suit growling about how "investing is serious business, harrumph." It was as though TD Waterhouse was above the fray the entire time and not filming the same get-rich-quick commercials that everyone else was. Broker, please.

Fast-forward 10 years, and the online brokerage business has matured quite a bit. These firms are no longer grasping at a growing pie; they are now drawing blood among themselves for a bigger slice of what's already out there. Trading commissions are in the mid-single digits across the board, and market share is everything. Schwab now boasts 8.1 million active accounts, while E*TRADE has 4.3 million. Ameritrade customers have some $420 billion in assets, with the firm executing an average of 373,000 trades per day. Growth has leveled off, and the bigger players have gotten really big.

There is still a sense of fun in the marketing (who doesn't love the E*TRADE Baby?), but as the industry has matured, most of it now focuses on the more pragmatic aspects of the firms. All the online brokers are now providing enhanced suites of tools, some useful (built-in retirement calculators) and some absurd (heat mapping, anyone?). This arms race has led to quite a bit of consolidation, as most of the upstart specialty brokers like Think or Swim and Options-Xpress have been snapped up in a steady succession of deal making.

While many of the players have merged, the survivors have since broadened out their business lines to include asset management, online banking, and even custody services for investment advisors like me. In my current financial advisory practice, I work with both Schwab and TD—my former archenemies from when they were wrecking the margins of full-service brokers with race-to-zero commission rates.

Between the decimalization of stock prices (we used to trade them in fractions and capture big spreads) and the onslaught of the online brokers, transactions are barely commissionable anymore. The processing of trades is now a no-margin business, with companies like Zecco offering buy and sell transactions at a commission rate of zero dollars per.

Discount brokers Fidelity, Schwab, E*TRADE, and TD Ameritrade are now making a fortune as they cater to the RIA vertical. Independent-minded advisors and "breakaway brokers" who leave the Merrills and Morgans need a brokerage firm to custody their client assets, and who better to fill those shoes than the discount brokers themselves. The irony here is delicious: Margin-wrecking online brokers force their full-service brokerage competition into the advisory business when transactional commissions become commoditized. These newly minted advisors leave their traditional brokerage firms and begin custodying assets with their former competitors, the online brokers. The scorched-earth campaign on commissions waged by the online discounters has paid off for them in spades.

One final aside on the destruction of commission brokerage; this one comes to us from the storied *Annals of Unintended Consequences*:

While retail investors have benefited greatly from the low- or no-commission revolution, one should consider the broader effects it has had on the financial industry and, by extension, the U.S. economy as a whole. By the late 1990s, it became obvious to the bulge bracket brokerage firms that buying and selling stock for retail clients would no longer be a viable growth business for them. As most of the wirehouse brokerages were owned by investment banks anyway, the inevitable and perhaps subconscious decision was made to develop more in-house products to push through their massive brokerage sales forces.

As a result, one of the key unintended consequences of the zeroing out of full-service commissions has been an explosion of structured products and other questionable wares. These would include a smorgasbord of banking deals, mortgage bonds, and other securitized debt instruments, reverse convertibles, auction rate securities, variable annuities, principal protection funds, unit investment trusts, in-house mutual funds, and other things that go bump in the night. When brokers could no longer charge 2 and 3 percent on generic stock trades anymore, they simply turned to these other lucrative lines of business. In doing so, they created a positively *systemic* amount of collateral damage. With their traditional brokerage profit centers under siege by online discounters, Wall Street firms also got themselves more heavily involved in derivatives, real estate, leveraged loans, mortgage under-writing and securitization, and even *tax-evasion-as-a-service.*

By driving the costs out of trading, the online brokerages had inadvertently driven the investment banks back to the profit draw-ing board—as history has shown time and again, Wall Street getting creative is almost never a good thing.

9

Unity Creates Strength

As we have previously discussed in Chapter 2, war bonds were the gateway drug that got everyday Americans in the investing mode, a minor tremor that gave rise to a few score brokerage firms in the early part of the twentieth century. The earthquake would eventually come along in the form of the mutual fund, America's most dominant investing instrument to this day.

The basic mutual fund structure has evolved over time; in its most primitive form, it resembled its slightly deformed cousin, the closed-end fund. The first recorded instance of an investment fund that opened up to attract the public involved a Dutch merchant named Adriaan van Ketwich in 1774. He called his fund *Eendragt Maakt Magt*, meaning "Unity Creates Strength." Fifty years later, King William I of the Netherlands would run with that concept as his nation sought more efficient ways of capitalizing its vast shipping and merchant enterprises. He launched what would today be described as a closed-end fund, which allowed for the public to take part in the rapidly industrializing economy around them.

Throughout the nineteenth century, many such funds would be created in Switzerland, Scotland, England, and France. The concept would make its way to America's shores in 1893 with the launch of the Boston Personal Property Trust, followed by Philadelphia's Alexander Fund in 1907.

In 1928, a year before the mass speculation of the Roaring Twenties would culminate in disaster, several major developments occurred which led to the dominance of the open-end fund, or mutual fund, in its modern form. But let's back up a bit to the early part of that decade as the post–World War I boom in American investing was just getting under way.

The year is 1924, and new inventions and postwar inflation are revolutionizing the way Americans treat their surplus capital. Beginning in 1923, the gross national product is growing at a rate of 4.2 percent, a rapid rate even for our time but an absolute *warp zone* for folks back then (see Figure 9.1).

Electric utilities are spreading across the nation, and widespread adoption of the appliances that rely on them means big bucks for manufacturers and retailers alike. Cars and trucks are popping up everywhere, as are the modern surfaced roadways and service stations they require. Ordinary people see what's happening around them, and like any rational beings, they want their cut of the action.

The trouble is, getting into the stock markets for most people is difficult, to say the least. The proliferation of bucket shops makes it so that it is very hard to trade fairly with The Street. The atmosphere at the large houses is equally clubby; there is very little interest on the part of the brokers in catering to those with only average fortunes

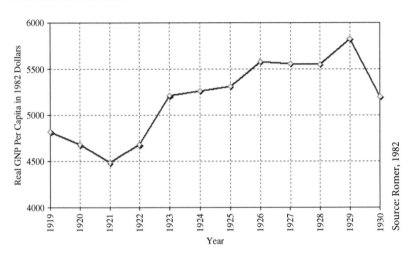

Figure 9.1. *Real GNP per Capita, 1919–1930*

to invest. In addition, a single share of General Electric is selling for $232 in 1924—roughly $2,900 per share in today's dollars!

With barriers like these, many ordinary investors go the closed-end fund route in the 1920s; there are about 700 funds to choose from by this time.

But that same year, the Massachusetts Investors' Trust will launch the first ever mutual fund. It's groundbreaking feature of daily liquidity for those looking to cash out or buy in, coupled with professional management and diversification, sets it apart from its closed-end fore-bears. It will begin sending out regular and comprehensive reports to its shareholders, a novelty during that time. It will also have the first in-house research department. Here is the *Boston Globe* rhapsodizing about the innovative new investment company on July 16, 1926:

> *The Massachusetts Investors Trust, organized in 1924 to afford the investor an opportunity to purchase a broad list*

of sound common stocks in convenient units, has grown in the interim from $50,000 paid in to more than $2,5 000,000 [sic] and now numbers just short of 1000 shareholders. Its funds are invested in the common stocks of 136 leading American corporations. The trustees have acquired the holdings of common stocks for permanent investment, not for speculation. Their selection to date has show [sic] the following interesting results: Of the 136 stocks held, three have passed their dividends, paid extras, or stock dividends or issued results. The result of market fluctuations has been equally favorable. At today's market, 26 of the 136 stocks are selling at less than they cost, but the other 110 issues are selling for enough more so that the value of the trust shares is more than 10 points above the offering price of 52-1/2.

By 1928, the Massachusetts Investors' Trust had created quite a name for itself. Its value-oriented style and predilection for blue chips over highfliers (yes, there were high-flying stocks even then) had appealed to the crowd that wanted to be in the markets but not overly at risk, as they feared having a brokerage account might lead to. Its "open-ended" fund architecture had inspired several imitators along the way. The first no-load fund will also be launched in 1928 by a group including Richard Scudder (name ring a bell?). Wellington will launch a fund that owns both bonds and stocks (what we'd call a balanced fund today), and State Street Bank, a modern-day fund giant, will break from just custodying fund assets and launch a retail product of its own that year. The year 1928 is the *big bang* year for the mutual fund industry, and enterprising young men around the nation are paying attention.

One of them, Phillip Carret, would go on to be one of the most important figures in the history of stock market investing. Carret studied chemistry at Harvard and enlisted in the Army Signal Corp (the original Air Force) in 1917. By the time his flight training was complete, the war in France had ended, and so he came back to the states and began selling bonds. He would end up being hired by Clarence Barron in Boston as a financial journalist for the *Barron's* financial magazine (yes, that *Barron's*). Then one day, Sherman Adams, founding trustee of the Massachusetts Investors' Trust, would walk into Barron's offices and begin talking about his newest mutual fund creation.

Carret rounds up every dollar he can from his family and friends ($25,000) and launches the Fidelity Investment Trust, unrelated to the Fidelity that exists today. He will ultimately rename it the Pioneer Fund, and like Sherman Adams's mutual fund, he will invest in such blue chips as Firestone Tire & Rubber and Maytag. Phil Carret will live until the age of 101, passing away during a hip replacement surgery in 1998. An interesting side note—he became great friends with Warren Buffett's father, Howard Buffett, when he visited the Omaha-based stockbroker in the 1940s. The two of them went on to bat around value ideas in the stock market on a regular basis for years to come.

Open-end funds are referred to as *Boston funds* in these early days. There are 19 of them by the market's crescendo top in 1929. When the crash rocks the nation, it is the hundreds of closed-end funds that pay the ultimate price. Many closed-ends are highly leveraged, and because they trade on the open market like stocks, they end up being wiped out and taking their investors' capital with them. Mutual funds like the Massachusetts Investors' Trust and Pioneer are also susceptible to the crash in stock prices and investor redemptions, but because they are not leveraged with debt and have been more disciplined than their rivals in the closed-end arena, they weather the storm and come into the 1930s' recovery in position for the massive shift that is about to occur.

By the early 1950s, there will be 100 different mutual funds available for the first time. In 1954, the stock market will finally eclipse its 1929 peak; and another 50 funds will come along, followed by another 100 in the 1960s—these of a more aggressive stripe.

In the 1970s, Wells Fargo creates the first index fund, another game-changing development in the now multi-billion-dollar investment management industry. Jack Bogle will take this index concept and drive internal costs down into the ground to build his Vanguard family of funds. He will revolutionize the fund industry and become an icon of cost management and investor pragmatism in his own right.

Joe Nocera, writing years ago for *Money* and *Fortune* magazines, quantifies the industry's growth for us during its peak years in the 1990s, also considered the baby boomers' peak earning and investing years. He notes that by 1994, 34 percent of American households have money in the market, up from only 10 percent in the 1950s. We're talking about hundreds of billions by 1995. Describing an Investment Company Institute conference that comes off more Roman orgy (Peking duck for 400!) than it does industry confab, Nocera captures the zeitgeist of the time perfectly in an article for *Fortune* from June 26, 1995:

> *These are standard answers to standard questions, but then comes the curve ball: Where will the Dow be in the year 2000, and how big will the mutual fund industry be? The pessimists—PESSIMISTS!—say that the Dow will go to 5000 by the turn of the century, and that the fund*

industry will grow by an additional trillion dollars. The most optimistic—Jessica Bibliowicz of Smith Barney, as it happens—predicts a 6500 Dow. She predicts the mutual fund industry will be managing more than $5 trillion by then. In other words, she thinks the industry will double over the next five years. Then again, why would she think anything else? Ms. Bibliowicz is 35 years old. The last time the mutual fund business endured a sustained bear market, she was 14.

By the year 2000, there is more cash in mutual funds than there is in the entire U.S. banking system. There are also more mutual funds than there are stocks on the New York Stock Exchange and NASDAQ markets combined. Investors, fueled by the promise of the twin technological wonders of wireless and Web as well as Alan Greenspan's interest rate largesse, have completely lost their minds by this point. They will pay the price in the next two years as the popular NASDAQ index and most of the funds invested in it will decline by some 80 percent—and this is before the chain of disasters that will include the demise of Enron and WorldCom followed by 9/11.

Everyone is in, and everyone is crushed.

The turn of the millennium marked the end of an 18-year secular bull market in equities. By 2001, 50 percent of American households were exposed to the stock market, mainly through the mutual funds in their 401(k) plans. This also marked the peak of the mutual fund industry, as the total number of funds would top out at 8,305 in 2001. While mutual funds remain a dominant investment vehicle to this day, their previously unquestioned status is now under more scrutiny than ever before. We are over a decade into a bear market during which stock prices have fluctuated greatly, with little forward progress, and investors are now asking the tough questions. These include:

- ○ "Why am I paying fees for active management?"
- ○ "How are these fees being charged, and what are my real costs?"
- ○ "What are the odds that I will be able to identify the small group of managers who will actually beat their benchmarks each year?"

The reality is that the fund industry really doesn't have any great answers to these questions, nor do the brokers who so lucratively sell so many funds to their clients each year.

10

Wholesalers and the Brokers Who Love Them

Ⅰt is 9:15 in the morning on a snowy day in the winter of 2003, and I haven't had my coffee just yet. Or I did but I'm cranky anyway. I am working in the Helmsley Building on Park Avenue and 45th Street in Manhattan. It has been designated a "landmark building," which really means that you'll have to pardon the building for the arctic office temps in the winter and the equatorial humidity in the summer. As I sit there dialing the phone, in the shadow of the gargantuan MetLife Building, which we all expect to be bombed any minute, I see an incoming call from a 617 area code. Boston. Here we go . . .

"Hello, this is Josh Brown."

"Hi Josh, Bill O'Shaughnessey from Fidelity.* How's yah day going?"

"Ya know, it's kinda just starting. Is there any way I can call you back?"

"Josh, I just wanted to touch base about our Select Biotechnology fund. Mahningstar has it ranked in the top decile for the last two quahters, and I really think it's worth a look for your clients."

"Yeah, I'm sure it's great, but I really gotta get my day going, the market's about to open up and . . ."

"No problem, Josh. Tell you what. My external sales rep James MacDougall's gonna be in Midtown on Mahch the 21st through the twenty-fawth. Can we put something on the calendah so I can get him in there to see you guys?"

"See which guys?"

"You and the rest of the brokers."

"They're all nitwit stock jockeys. They don't want to meet anyone except Gordon Gekko, and I'm pretty sure he's a fictional character. Your external James would be wasting his time here."

"How about if Fidelity buys you guys lunch. They'll sit through a few slides for that, right?"

---

* There is no Bill O'Shaughnessey; he is a construct based on several dozen internals I have dealt with over the years. And I don't mean to pick on Fidelity here; the guys at the Fidelity Advisor Funds were absolutely fantastic to work with during my brokerage days. In fact, I didn't write this chapter to go after any fund company in particular. All the funds use similar sales tactics for the broker channel, and most of their people tend to be hardworking and smart.

"Now you're talking. Pizza from Naples 45 buys you 20 minutes. Anything longer than that, and we're talking sandwiches from Cucina."

"Tell ya what. Let's do that Wednesday. We'll make the catering arrangements the day before."

"Fine, thanks, Bill. I gotta hop . . ."

"Great! Before you go, let me just confirm your e-mail, fax number, mailing address . . ."

"Yeah, guy, I have clients to call back . . ."

"OK, no worries. I'll just give you a buzz this afternoon to check in. We can go over the fact sheet on that New York municipal select I sent you last week . . ."

"Oh my god, please. I'll buy any fund you want, I swear, just make it stop."

If brokers are the most aggressive and tenacious salespeople on the planet, then imagine the guys and gals responsible for selling stuff to the brokers themselves. You have no idea. The call I've just narrated is a pretty faithful amalgam of a few hundred just like it I've been on over the years.

Every broker-sold mutual fund family has a pretty serious and regimented sales apparatus to make sure the brokers in each territory are hearing their "stories." On The Street, brokers call stocks "stories," but the wholesalers call themes and individual funds "stories." "Fairy tales" would be a more apt term as I would come to learn, but we'll get there in a few moments.

So here is how the wholesaler-broker connection works. Pay attention here, because if you have a 401(k) with load funds in it or an IRA at a brokerage firm, this will go a long way toward explaining how your current fund portfolio has come to be.

The wholesalers work for the fund family. Their job is to speak with the brokerage firms in their territories as often as possible without pissing anyone off (mission unaccomplished). There is both an internal wholesaler and an external wholesaler who cover the brokers in each territory or region.

Internals are the ones making the phone calls and sending the e-mails. They are distributing the literature on the various fund offerings and also those "think" pieces that justify never selling anything. The funds don't get paid their fees when investors go to cash, and so almost every investment company produces the infamous "10 Best Days" brochure. This brochure will say something like "The S&P 500 has returned 300 percent in the last 15 years—but if you were out of the market during the 10 best days, you only saw an 80 percent return." I'm exaggerating, but you know what I mean. My partner Barry Ritholtz has actually done the math on this most specious of marketing myths. It turns out that if you missed the 10 worst days, you did even better than the chumps who were worried about being fully invested the whole way through. Anyway, that's the kind of stuff the internals pump out all day.

They also take incoming calls from the brokers they cover and tend to be extremely knowledgeable about their products and very helpful. Over the years, I've had great working relationships with many of them from BlackRock to Fidelity to Pimco. The trouble is, they all have phone extensions off the 800 number with six digits, and they tend to get rotated to different territories a lot. You call up one day, and the person who answers is all like, "Oh yeah, Patrick is covering the greater Delaware area, but my name's Marissa. Can I help you?" And I'm all like, "Not really. I kind of want my dear, sweet Patrick to walk me through something." Oh, well.

The external wholesaler is the internal's sidekick. Or vice versa. I actually believe that externals get paid more, and to me they have the much more arduous job of the two. The internal is constantly setting up appointments for his or her external partner to go out and see brokers who should be selling more of their funds to clients. The external has to have a much more extensive and snazzy wardrobe than the internal, because he or she is banging through different brokerages and banks all day long. The external is the person doing the talking while the brokers chow down on whatever catering was brought in for the due diligence meeting.

Often a giant cardboard box full of literature and sales material will be shipped over to the branch a day or two prior to the external's arrival. I used to jokingly warn the brokers not to open up the box until the sales rep from the fund company got there or else the rep would put the dreaded *wholesaler's curse* on us, and it would be seven years of bad luck. The brokers would look at me with blank stares like I was some kind of an idiot and then they'd get back to their phones. Anyway, the external comes in and does the usual dog and pony show. The brokers ask a handful of questions just to be polite, a few of them sleep through it behind sunglasses, and I usually squirt Dijon mustard out of a packet onto my tie. The whole thing is a waste of time if the guys don't drop at least $100,000 worth of tickets on the fund within a day or so. They almost never did.

And if this all sounds futile to you, keep in mind that it's only gotten worse with the advent of exchange-traded funds and the growing realization that active management is a farce anyway. And I've only been describing the scene at a small or regional broker-dealer; the draconian process of getting in to see a large wirehouse sales force is unimaginable. A Midtown Manhattan branch of a Smith Barney or a Merrill Lynch could have seven or eight of these externals in their offices every day of the week. They all sit in the waiting room with their attaché cases on their laps, pretending to scroll through e-mails on their BlackBerries as they await the precious 15 minutes they may be granted by the Thundering Herd. It all sounds horrible until they crack in. And then it's absolute nirvana for the wholesaler, who will be paid on tens of millions, even hundreds of millions, in assets coming his way. The thing about wirehouse guys is that they're resistant to change of any kind; once they start using a product, it tends to stay in their repertoire forever. When you get your fund into that regular rotation, the steam shovel of incoming cash is unstoppable.

The fund family is regulated under the Investment Company Act of 1940. Either the fund families are managing your money themselves using in-house research (like Janus or T. Rowe Price), or they are simply marketing a fund under their own name but using subadvisors to actually handle the investing (like John Hancock, the insurance broker, tends to do).

Either way, the name of the game is assets under management, and the fund families usually offer several share classes in order to entice different brokers to sell their funds to you. I'll give you a very basic description of the major share classes and how they work:

A *shares.* A full commission is charged up front, beginning at as high as 5.75 percent and sliding down, based on how much you put in (a breakpoint discount). The broker is paid that day by the fund family. The negative is that you start off 5 percent in the hole on day one. The positive (and I use that term loosely) is that your shares are free and clear to be sold immediately with no penalty and there are no trailing commissions eating into your ongoing returns above and beyond the fund's internal expense ratio.

B *shares.* These are basically the devil. A broker who sells you B shares is either a dirtbag or he just hates you or he truly doesn't know any better. B shares offer the broker a similar commission percentage as A shares, but instead of the commission being deducted from your principal on day one, it is surreptitiously paid to the broker from the fund company itself so that you start out with 100 percent of your money invested from Jump Street. Sounds great, right? OK, but if you sell within the first couple of years, you get nailed for that commission on the way out. Plus, the returns are dampened by ongoing 12b-1 fees used for marketing expenses so the fund can bring in more investors. It's not until six years have passed that your B shares convert into A shares and you're able to sell with no penalty. As if any of us will even be alive in six years once the nuclear war between Google and Facebook turns the country into a war-ravaged apocalypse. Anyway, the B-share class has become so demonized that many brokerage firms are no longer allowing employees to sell them, and the fund companies themselves have actually ceased offering them. A well-deserved extinction to be sure.

C shares. The C-share fund is as close as you get to having a broker try to get paid and still do the right thing by the client. C shares are far from perfect, but they do align the broker's compensation a bit more with the client's success. The C share pays the broker a 1 percent fee the day he or she buys the fund for you and then a 1 percent trailing commission for each year you hold onto it until infinity. This arrangement does dampen performance over time (as any fee will), but the broker is betting on a long-term relationship with you and will have more upside based on the success of the fund (the higher your assets climb, the more his or her 1 percent trailer will translate into). Before leaving the brokerage business, I was doing C-share business almost exclusively whenever using open-end mutual funds. It was the most like an advisor I was able to be at the time even though I was, in the words of my broker colleagues, "leaving mad gross on the table." Those assholes are probably waiting tables these days, so whatever.

Now there are also things like I-class shares (the lowest-cost class, for large institutional purchasers) and T-class shares (some convoluted hybrid between the A and the C), but we won't get carried away here.

The point I'd like to leave you with is that, other than the brokers, no one has the slightest idea how these things are actually charging them. Nobody has a clue how much the salesperson is making from each class or what the true cost to the clients is over time. And we're not just talking about brokerage clients either. If you work at a company where the 401(k) plan was pitched to the owners by a brokerage firm, you likely have A or C shares as your sole options. This means you are paying the brokers who set the company plan up with a cooperating fund family; they are carving up the fees from your fund elections each month despite the fact that you've never met any of them. The funny part is, the brokers have really only selected the plan's choices at the very beginning; in many cases, there is no ongoing maintenance from that point, merely the collection of trailing fees.

And before we move on, there's one other thing you may want to be aware of when looking at the composition of your brokerage account and the fund choices in it. There's a very good chance that the fund family has actually paid your broker just to be on the platform. One of the most insidious and unknown practices on The Street is called the *revenue-sharing agreement*. Rather than take pains to explain it, I'll give it to you directly from the horse's mouth. The following appears on the Web site of one of the largest brokerage firms in the country on a page called "Revenue-Sharing

Fund Families," I've redacted the name and edited it down to make my point:

> *The following revenue-sharing information pertains to mutual fund purchases in commission-based brokerage accounts . . .*
>
> *From each fund family offered, [Redacted Brokerage Firm Name] seeks to collect a mutual fund support fee, or what has come to be called a revenue-sharing payment. These revenue-sharing payments are in addition to the sales charges, annual distribution and service fees (referred to as "12b-1 fees"), applicable redemption fees and deferred sales charges, and other fees and expenses disclosed in the fund's prospectus fee table . . .*
>
> *Set forth below is a listing of the fund families from which we received revenue-sharing payments in 2009. Fund families are listed in descending order based upon the total amount of revenue-sharing payments we recognized from each fund family for 2009 . . .*

In other words, this is a classic pay-to-play racket. "You want access to our client cash, you gotta sweeten the pot, boys." The firms have to disclose this stuff somewhere, and I'm certain it's not located in the "Dear Investor" welcome letter!

Brokers and fund wholesalers are forever engaged in an ongoing dance, with your retirement assets as the music playing in the background. As of 2010, 54 percent of all 401(k) and 403(b) retirement assets were invested in mutual funds, as were 47 percent of all IRA assets. I thought you'd like to know how they got there.

11

The Feeling Is Mutual

We've talked about how mutual funds came to dominate the investment industry and about how fund families work with brokers to get you in and keep you in at all times. I use mutual funds on a daily basis for getting my clients exposure to areas of the market or strategies that I simply cannot provide on my own with the same level of diversification or expertise. The mark of a true financial advisor is knowing when to bring in outside managers on a client's behalf, even if it means sharing fees. There is a misconception among some advisors that this somehow diminishes them in the clients' eyes. It does no such thing. In fact, this willingness to employ the talents of others to help clients reach their goals can only elevate an advisor's standing to the only people who count—the customers.

While certain types of mutual funds have become indispensable to me, I am far from enamored with the industry as a whole. As a matter of fact, I've come to believe that a majority of mutual funds have no reason to exist at all in this day and age. There are too many better and lower-cost options. It is incomprehensible to me that there was still some $11.8 trillion in assets held in over 7,500 mutual funds by the investing public as of the end of 2010.

Granted this total number of assets includes roughly $2.7 trillion in money market (cash) funds, but this is a still a remarkable total for an industry that hasn't justified having so much stewardship over our investment dollars. There are four main reasons why the mutual fund complex still has possession over so much capital despite the existence of many superior alternatives:

1. *Inertia.* Sir Isaac Newton, while a terrible investor, understood a thing or two about physics. His idea that "bodies at rest tend to remain at rest" has perhaps never been truer than when applied to the typical fund investor. Many self-directed investors will only sell a mutual fund when they have an actual need for the cash, while many broker-assisted investors don't see their funds turned over until the broker has decided that it's time to earn a new commission.

2. *Retirement assets.* Mutual funds absolutely own the retirement market. They enjoy a virtual monopoly on the 401(k) racket that Vito Corleone himself would salivate over. On the distant horizon, there is some danger of exchange-traded funds (ETFs) making inroads, but this is still a long way off. As of the end of 2009, the nation's 401(k) plans had nearly $2.7 billion in ETFs, says research firm BrightScope. This amount is a joke in the context of the total defined benefit plan asset pool of $4.5 trillion.

3. *Broker preference.* If brokers sell their clients an exchange-traded fund, the brokers will be able to charge only the typical

percentage commission they get for a stock transaction (these days between 1 and 2 percent). They will not receive any trailing fees after that in an era of vigilance against churning accounts; it's not like they can sell that ETF so quickly afterward. All things being equal, it becomes more profitable to sell clients a mutual fund, either an A-share product with a big up-front load or some other class that keeps the trailing commissions coming in every quarter. Until the brokerage business flips to an all-advisory model, this won't change.

4. *Marketing.* The sales and advertising prowess of the mutual fund industry is rivaled solely by the brokerage firm business in the selling of a financial product that only actually "works" in rare instances if ever at all. Given that every year 80 percent of mutual funds fall short of the S&P 500's benchmark return, we can do nothing other than raise our glasses to the marketing geniuses who keep the coffers full at fund families across the country. Bravo, ladies and gentlemen, you've outdone yourselves!

To understand the love affair between people and their mutual funds, we have to look at the most recent bull market and the wealth effect it created for the investor class. Americans had been spoiled by a stock market run that began in 1982 during which every dip was a buying opportunity and every well-known company in America was also a winning stock investment. Coca-Cola, Pfizer, Johnson & Johnson, McDonald's, and IBM were all among the best performers of the era, which was convenient for most investors in that these were the companies they already knew. In fact, "Buy what you know" became the central meme of this period, a quasi-religion of sorts complete with the ritualistic buying and holding of blue chips (large-cap stocks) and blue chip stock funds.

The mutual fund industry was perhaps the biggest beneficiary of America's worshipful devotion to blue chip stocks during the 1980s and 1990s. In 1982, mutual funds held $300 billion in investor assets. Just five years later, that total had more than doubled to $715 billion. By the end of the 1990s, this total had increased tenfold to $6.84 trillion!

Now every religion has a messiah, and the 1982 to 2000 stock craze was no exception. While there were many well-regarded investment gurus during the bull run, Peter Lynch so perfectly embodied the spirit of that feel-good moment that there are some who still refer to those days as the Peter Lynch era. Lynch joined Fidelity investments as the director of research in the early 1970s and in 1977 was handed the keys to the Fidelity Magellan Fund, a little-known mutual fund with only $20 million in assets under management. By 1990, Magellan had grown into a $20 billion behemoth through a combination of Lynch's stellar returns and Fidelity's own top-flight marketing savvy.

The Peter Lynch investment philosophy would be laid out for all to read in two of the greatest investment books ever written: 1989's *One Up on Wall Street,* in which Lynch explained his investing methodology, and 1993's *Beating the Street,* which was about applying his methods toward making actual investments. The books flew off the shelves almost as quickly as investment dollars poured in over the transom. Boston-based Fidelity was awash in cash during one of the greatest bull markets in history, as Peter Lynch's plain-English message to investors proved irresistible to the masses. Looking at the core tenets of his philosophy, one can understand why they proved so popular to a generation that was just entering its peak earning and investing years. Investopedia sums up Lynch's eight principles of stock selection from a talk he gave in 2005:

o Know what you own.

o It's futile to predict the economy and interest rates.

- You have plenty of time to identify and recognize exceptional companies.
- Avoid long shots.
- Good management is very important—buy good businesses.
- Be flexible and humble, and learn from mistakes.
- Before you make a purchase, you should be able to explain why you're buying.
- There's always something to worry about.

Lynch also preached the gospel of buy and hold, a concept that investors became equally devoted to as it continued to reward them year after year. He once remarked that "Absent a lot of surprises, stocks are relatively predictable over twenty years. As to whether they're going to be higher or lower in two to three years, you might as well flip a coin to decide."

The core of Lynch's message was that you, yes *you*, can do it. "If you stay half-alert, you can pick the spectacular performers right from your place of business or out of the neighborhood shopping mall, and long before Wall Street discovers them," he told his growing audience of admirers and acolytes. Armed with this encouragement that anyone could find great investing opportunities by simply paying attention to trends and products at the local mall, investors began to play the game for themselves. This wave of mass stock market participation meant big business for the various fund families, which had rock-star managers to market to the public.

His "buy what you know" and "think long-term" message was later bastardized and misinterpreted as "name brand stocks will always work" and "never sell." But as the tech boom began to make stars out of previously obscure companies and as high-octane traders hijacked the market from slower investors, this message would ultimately come to be ridiculed as a quaint and outdated way of thinking. This is a shame, as Peter Lynch's record as Magellan's manager still stands as the most remarkable in the history of the mutual fund industry. In the footnotes of his revised edition of *The Intelligent Investor*, finance journalist and author Jason Zweig reminds us of just how amazing Lynch truly was:

> The highest 20-year return in mutual fund history was 25.8% per year, achieved by the legendary Peter Lynch of Fidelity Magellan over the two decades ending December 31st 1994. Lynch's performance turned $10,000 into more than $982,000 in 20 years.

While other fund managers have gone on notable streaks, nobody can touch Peter Lynch's run—not before, during, or since.

Unfortunately for the ordinary investors, the mutual fund industry simply isn't brimming over with superstars like Lynch. In fact, managers of his caliber are one in a million and more likely to be found in the higher-reward hedge fund industry nowadays. This dearth of talent is only now starting to be noticed by the public, as people's returns in many cases are below those of the benchmarks over the past decade.

Not only are there no more Peter Lynch-esque managers in the mutual fund complex, but these days it seems like some of our generation's most storied managers are in a race to tarnish their long-term track records. Bill Gross, the legendary manager of the world's largest mutual fund (Pimco's Total Return), has been very vocal about his distaste for U.S. Treasurys at their current yield. While his logic is unassailable, his bet against them (via short sales) has thus far kept him trailing the benchmarks he used to beat in his sleep.

Bill Miller of the Legg Mason Value Trust is the only mutual fund manager in history to have beaten the S&P 500 for 15 years straight. He has fed this superlative into a wood chipper since his streak ended in 2005, with only one year since then in which he's beaten his peers and three years of trailing the benchmark itself. Managers like Miller have the unfortunate burden of taking in a huge amount of assets just as they're coming off a long winning streak. They are doomed to be a disappointment almost no matter what they do, as performance-chasing investors scrutinize their every stock pick. As an example, Miller's June 2011 sale of Eastman Kodak shares at 3 after having bought a huge slug of the stock at 53 a decade ago was ridiculed mercilessly in the financial media.

The Fairholme Fund offers another example of a manager taking in big money just as his hot streak is ending. Fairholme, like Legg Mason Value Trust, is a value-oriented fund with concentrated positions and an iconic manager, in this case Bruce Berkowitz. Berkowitz was named Mutual Fund Manager of the Decade for the 10 years ending in 2009, and his performance had trounced nearly the entire field. His Fairholme Fund would balloon up to over $30 billion in assets under management as investors "chased the hot dot" right to his doorstep. Unfortunately Fairholme's market-beating returns seemed to disappear just as a maximum amount of inflows had poured in. Berkowitz is currently fighting a nasty PR battle as both investors and the media question his wisdom in making big bets on several companies with disastrous fundamentals like Citigroup, Bank of America, and a Florida land company called St. Joe. His bets may yet pay off, but they've already cost him several quarters of massive underperformance, not to mention a boatload of shareholder angst. The Fairholme Fund was down 27 percent through the first 10 months of 2011 versus its peer group's roughly flat performance.

But while consistently beating the market is the holy grail of the mutual fund complex, failing to do so is the reality. One of the first statisticians who looked at this paradox was Alfred Cowles, a Yale-educated researcher who studied investment returns back in the 1930s. He formed the Cowles Commission, a research outfit dedicated to debunking the market-beating claims of the era. If he were alive now, he'd be number one on Wall Street's Most Wanted list and persona non grata in the Boston financial district. Cowles would publish the landmark article "Can Stock Market Forecasters Forecast?" in 1932. His precise measurements of the results of stock forecasters and those who made market-timing calls were damning evidence indeed. Cowles concludes that, in reality, only one-third of these analysts could pick stocks that beat the market over a five-year period. He answers the question that his article posits with a simple "It is doubtful."

In the modern era, no one has been more vocal about the inferiority of actively managed funds versus their passive peers than Vanguard's John Bogle. Bogle's contrary (if biased) take on the actively managed fund industry is one of the few that has ever been heard above the cacophony of marketing noise. There is one statistic that he and his faction want every investor to be aware of. In his 1998 book *Common Sense on Mutual Funds: New Imperatives for the Intelligent Investor*, we are told that around 80 percent of all mutual fund managers fail to even *meet* the return of the S&P 500 every year, let alone exceed it. This inconvenient truth would be a dagger in the heart of the fund industry—if only the industry weren't so good at misdirecting our attention elsewhere.

While it's true that the appeal of the mutual fund has diminished over the last 10 years, the industry is still very much alive and well. This despite the fact that lower-cost ETFs have become the more widely accepted vehicle for index exposure and have gotten extremely creative about covering niches in the market that mutual funds are just not suited for. With Vanguard, Pimco, and several other large devotees of the open-end fund now creating ETF versions of their popular mutual funds, it is safe to say that the writing is on the wall. But while the fund industry is currently in the throes of this massive transition, it is important to understand that traditional mutual funds are still scaling new heights in terms of assets under management, albeit at a much slower pace than before.

12

Your Fellow Fund Shareholders

If the majority of mutual funds are unable to do what their marketing professes they can, who is it that keeps throwing their money at these things? Good question.

According to the Investment Company Institute (ICI), mutual funds now account for 20 percent of all American households' financial assets. ICI reports that "between mid-year 1989 and mid-year 2010, assets held in mutual funds have increased from $899 billion to $10.5 trillion. The number of U.S. households that owned mutual funds rose from 23.2 million to 51.6 million over the same period." ICI goes on to tell us that "as of mid-year 2010, 43.9 percent of U.S. households owned mutual funds, representing 90.2 million individual mutual fund shareholders."

Using data from 2010, we see that typical mutual fund investors are middle aged, employed, and married. They are making about

$80,000 a year, and their household net worth is in the neighborhood of $200,000. Mutual funds make up about half of their portfolios. They also tend to have some kind of a retirement account, like a 401(k) or an IRA. The 401(k) or other qualified plan account will be dominated by mutual funds unless the holder is the employee of a public corporation, in which case company stock will be a big part of the mix. The statistics show that:

- 68 percent of mutual fund–owning households will own them through 401(k) plans, but the sales channel outside of retirement accounts is still highly important to fund families.

- 72 percent of mutual fund investors will also own them outside of the plan.

- 58 percent of mutual fund–owning households have been sold their funds by brokers, financial planners, insurance agents, accountants, or bank employees.

- 36 percent—a smaller but still significant number of investors—have bought fund shares of their own volition, either directly from a mutual fund company or in their discount brokerage accounts.

As for income levels:

- 39 percent of households holding mutual funds had an income level somewhere between $50,000 and $99,000 by 2010.

- 21 percent of fund-owning households earned somewhere around $100,000 a year.

- 44 percent had assets of more than $250,000.

In other words, mutual fund investors make good customers for other investment products and services.

As can be expected, the majority of mutual fund households are headed by members of the baby-boomer generation. They've been treated well by their involvement with funds over the years, at least until the year 2000 when the bull market in stocks that began in 1982 came to an abrupt and shocking end. Even still, boomers make up 44 percent of fund-owning households, followed by the Gen Xers, who make up only 24 percent of the total. A big piece of the current mutual fund ownership pie consists of investors who first got involved with funds prior to 1990 (38 percent). Another large chunk of holders (21 percent) first bought mutual funds during the "Irrational Exuberance" Era between 1995 and 1999. Finally, 26 percent of fund investors have come in after the year 2000, and many of these have little or nothing to show for their purchases since stocks have essentially round-tripped during the last decade.

And now, much to the chagrin of the fund complex (and thousands of Boston Red Sox fans, thankfully), this dynasty over the investment business is coming to an end.

The fact that the boomers will be liquidating their equity funds over the next decade as they settle into retirement is lost on no one in the industry. About 58 percent of mutual fund–owning heads of household are between 40 and 64, and the median is tilting further toward 64 with every passing day. Boomers were the perfect buy-and-hold, bread-and-butter investors that mutual funds lived off for the last three decades. Fund families learned how to market to them and what made them tick. And now they are going away.

The first baby boomers were born in 1946 when the war ended and America's sailors and soldiers came home filled with, well, let's just say *spirit*. If you add 65 years to 1946, you arrive at 2011—which means the first boomers have just started to hit retirement age now. Beginning in January 2011, there were 10,000 boomers per day who started turning age 65. This will continue until the year 2030 or when the robots enslave us, whichever comes first (I'm betting robots).

According to statistics supplied before the U.S. House of Representatives by Vanguard's John Bogle, more than 30 percent of investors in their sixties have greater than 80 percent of their 401(k) invested in equities, most of which is through mutual funds. The fund families will not be able to count on these assets for much longer, as required minimum distributions trigger the redemptions that our ongoing bear market couldn't. Fixed-income funds will likely hold onto assets better than their equity fund cousins but with low rates. The mass exodus will leave no corner of the fund industry untouched. And while 40 percent of baby boomers surveyed by the AARP recently said they'd be working until they drop, the reality will probably turn out to be somewhat different.

In addition to the aging of their best customers, mutual funds face new competition from the nimbler ETF products that have been seeing stratospheric rates of growth and adoption regardless of market conditions. As more stockbrokers transition to the advisory model, less mutual funds will be sold to investors and more ETFs will be bought on their behalf (we'll be looking at the rise of the ETF model later on).

The bottom line is that while the total assets under management at mutual fund companies has never been higher, it is unlikely to grow much from current levels ever again. Demographics have a funny and unstoppable way of thwarting the best-laid plans of entire industries at times. This is one of those inevitable scenarios. What it will mean is ever-fiercer competition among the funds themselves. This will manifest itself in lower management fees, consolidation among the providers, a transitioning toward exchange-traded products, and the slow, steady decline of the once mighty product that ruled the American investment landscape for 70 years.

One thing I'll miss when the mutual funds begin to disappear is the marketing. It's all so adorable. Open up any financial magazine, and you feel as though you're walking through a carnival midway. There is fencing, juggling, and even a strong man hefting obscenely heavy objects to the delight of the crowd. There are exotic animals and all manner of outrageous claims being made in front of each tent on the fairgrounds.

And the names of the funds themselves! "Opportunity" and "Discovery" and "Endeavor"! Are these mutual funds or spaceships? "Our mission is to provide investors with . . ." A *mission*? I love missions! There are so many mutual fund types, it can all be disorienting, and so I've put together the chart in Table 12.1 to help you parse the various names and what they mean,

Now you may be saying to yourself, "But Josh, didn't you say earlier that you do use some mutual funds?" Why yes, yes I did. And while this isn't a "how to invest" book, there are a few things I'll mention in this regard.

There are certain styles and strategies that I simply cannot replicate on my own that I want my clients to have exposure to. As an investment advisor representative at a good-sized shop, I am able to purchase I-class (institutional class) mutual funds for my clients which carry the lowest possible internal expenses and have no brokerage fees or commissions associated with them. I suppose in some cases I could bring in an outside separately managed account (SMA) solution, but the fees of these SMAs are not much lower at most asset-level thresholds. And besides, I work with a handful of mutual funds that have done incredibly well in a variety of market environments, and so if the expenses are in line with other solutions, why mess with success?

The short list of mutual funds I tend to use consists of the multiasset-class, global allocation variety. My clients don't want me

Table 12.1

Fund Brochure Says . . .	What It Really Means . . .
Ultra	Leveraged to the hilt
Global growth	We'll chase stocks for you in whichever country is most overheated right now
Clean/green	A basket of government-subsidized experiments and some shares of GE
Deep value	We will invest in sewing machine and typewriter companies
Premium	We will pay up for high-multiple stocks/you will pay up in fees
Socially responsible	No such thing—all corporations are evil, sucker
Diversified	We will basically buy the index and go golfing
Enhanced	Uses exotic derivatives you've never heard of
Balanced	We will underperform both the bond and the stock market. You're welcome
Aggressive growth	Collection of Chinese online gaming stocks and New Jersey biotech start-ups
Life cycle	We can see 20 years into the future; only Putnam knows when and how you will die
Moderate allocation	Gutless fund manager
Quantitative	Manager will take credit for up years, blame computers for down years
Endeavor/opportunities	We will throw darts
Core	No need to spread it out; send us everything you have

trying to pick convertible bonds in Asia for them, nor do they want me making currency decisions between the Brazilian real and the Swiss franc. If I can bring in a powerhouse fund management team to do that and deploy their expertise on behalf of the clients I serve, everybody wins.

But these funds are few and far between. The vast majority of mutual funds are lucky to be alive in my estimation. There are thousands of them that serve no discernible purpose at this point.

We already know that most managers don't even meet the S&P 500's return in a given year, and let me assure you that the track records for the limitless number of sector funds are no more impressive versus the funds' own benchmarks. The reality is that most investors don't need exposure to one specific sector, and those who truly want it are almost always better off with a passive product like a sector ETF. You want exposure to the gold miners? Just buy the gold miner index. It's been my experience that most sector-fund managers are merely hugging their sector's benchmark anyway.

There are some sectors where stock picking is very important, such as biotechnology. Biotech stocks are the ultimate binary bets—total feast or famine. Now you might say to yourself that having a professional fund manager who reads all the clinical papers and talks to the doctors and knows the science would be a good guy to bet on. But no matter how skilled and knowledgeable that manager is, a fund holding 100 different biotech stocks is not going to give you enough exposure to the one or two big winners in the sector; your returns will be diluted by all the also-rans he or she has you invested in.

In general, if there is a trade to be had by being long or short a particular sector, then the ETF is a more efficient way of expressing the trade, certainly not the actively managed sector mutual fund. I predict that these funds will gradually disappear over the next few years.

And I don't mean to pick on sector funds exclusively; most actively managed foreign stock funds are equally pointless. Don't think that because a fund family has analysts in-country or "boots on the ground" that it will really matter—it won't over the long term. If you want overseas exposure, buy the low-cost country-specific fund or some kind of passive, fundamentally weighted index.

Wherever possible with overseas stock funds, I look for an equal-weighted option (as opposed to market cap–weighted). The reason I do this is that many developing countries end up with two or three mega-cap stocks that dominate the averages. A good case in point to illustrate this problem would be Brazil. The most commonly used vehicle for Brazilian exposure is not a mutual fund but a country-specific iShares ETF, ticker symbol EWZ. The problem with this index fund is that most of the holdings are overshadowed by exceedingly large positions in the country's big commodities exporters, Petrobras and Vale. Essentially, you end up with a portfolio that is highly levered to the prices of iron ore and oil, not the Brazilian economy. I've eschewed the EWZ fund and have opted for BRF, a more evenly distributed index of small- and mid-cap companies that tend to be a better play on the emerging Brazilian middle-class consumer. I see no need to bet on (and pay for) an active manager who may or may not "do a good job." If I want Brazil, I just buy Brazil, not a picker of Brazilian stocks.

As more investors come around to my way of thinking (and they will), the mutual fund complex will stop churning out actively managed mutual funds and will focus more on market analytics and quantitative methods of stock categorization. This will mean less mutual funds overall and many more ETFs. Costs will go down; so will profits for the investment companies, and some will be bought or die. But the options for both investors and their advisors will get even more specific and specialized. We'll look at the ETF market in the next chapter.

The Greatest Financial Innovation in 70 Years

It is the winter of 2002, and I'm sitting in the half-empty board-room of a hollowed-out brokerage firm. Investors had spent the past year pulling a net $27 billion from stock mutual funds. The broker-age industry has been utterly ravaged by the successive backbreaking events of the dot-com crash, 9/11, and that matched set of account-ing debacles, Enron and WorldCom. Fully half of the guys I came up with in the business had left by this point; they were off selling insurance or mortgages or whatever else was a more readily received proposition than common stocks. Now that widely held fallen angels like Cisco, Lucent, Sun Microsystems, Palm, and AOL Time Warner had broken all our hearts, the American public was disgusted with the stock market, and there was not a single exciting thing for us to talk about to turn the public around.

The Fed had cut rates to extraordinarily low levels, which was starting to be felt in the real estate market, but in Stockbrokerville we were just absolutely decimated. No one wanted to hear from us, period.

And into these ruins strode a heavyset man wearing a matching navy blue polo shirt and ball cap, each emblazoned with a spider logo. He had a box of sales literature under his arm. The partners had grudgingly given him this time to come in and make a presentation to our gutted sales force about an innovative new product that could possibly change our fortunes.

"Good afternoon, gents," the man said, as my fellow brokers barely looked up to acknowledge his presence. "I work for the American Stock Exchange, and I'm here to tell you guys about a brand-new way to invest your clients' money that's cheaper and more efficient than whatever you're doing now."

"Yeah, what's the commission? If it ain't 5 percent, you're in the wrong place, pal."

Amex Guy ignores the guido with the thick Brooklyn accent and the even thicker Gucci tie. "How many of you guys are familiar with the SPDR, or Spyder S&P fund, that trades like a stock?"

A few hands go up, and someone in the back of the room belches. You can hear clicking on keyboards as the apathy in the room manifests itself in the sound of Web surfing.

"Well, what if I told you that on the Amex, we're beginning to trade dozens of versions of the SPDR that will allow you to buy and sell entire indexes and specific sectors in a single trade?"

The keyboard clicking stops, and a few heads lift off the desks.

"What if I said that with a single order ticket you could be long or short the entire oil and gas sector rather than a specific stock? What if I told you there was a way to buy the entire NASDAQ 100 without using index options or an index mutual fund that locks your clients' money in?"

Now he had us. Those of us who were left, anyway. A liquid way to be in and out of the indexes without locking up client money in a mutual fund meant huge money in commissions for active trading accounts. It meant building positions for clients without exposing ourselves to single-stock risk. Amex Guy may have looked like a schlub, but he just pulled a Ferrari up to our driveway and handed us the keys.

"Do yourselves a favor and have a look at this list of the exchange-traded funds that are currently trading. There are way more of them now than just the S&P Spyder fund, and I'm telling you guys, this is the future. And here are some SPDR ball caps courtesy of the American Stock Exchange. You have a good night."

That was 10 years ago. That gentleman from the Amex wasn't kidding around. Though we only had an inkling at the time, these new ETFs would change everything. They would captivate the do-it-yourselfers and become the go-to option for the pros. They would wrench the vaunted mutual fund from its seemingly unassailable pedestal high above the investing landscape. They would go on to alter the very fabric of the capital markets themselves. The ETF would become the greatest financial innovation since the open-end mutual fund's genesis in 1924.

Structurally speaking, the ETF looks like a closed-end fund in that it is bought and sold all day on an exchange. But unlike the closed-end fund, which can and will trade at either a discount or a premium to its holdings at any given moment, the ETF is designed to trade to within pennies of its actual net asset value at all times. The goal is for the ETF to move about all day in concert with the basket of stocks or the index that it's supposed to replicate with as little "tracking error" as possible. It does this through a mechanism called *creation/redemption*, which we'll not get bogged down with here. Suffice it to say that the vast majority of plain-vanilla index and sector ETFs are extremely efficient in this regard.

Because the ETF's price is meant to accurately reflect its net asset value, it is more akin to the mutual fund—but with one major mechanical difference. ETFs offer all-day liquidity and can be bought and sold like a stock with no penalties or lingering consequences. In contrast, mutual fund investors must wait until the close of business for their buy and sell orders to be filled. Mutual funds can have all kinds of backdoor fees involved with selling, depending on what share class you're in and how long you hold the funds. The end result is that investors can be more nimble and fleet-footed when necessary with an ETF over a more traditional fund.

In terms of cost advantages, the ETF has every other investment company structure beat by a mile. It has a significantly lower expense ratio than the mutual fund because it doesn't have to invest cash contributions, fund cash redemptions, maintain reserves for redemptions, or pay big brokerage costs. Whereas mutual funds typically charge 1 to 3 percent on the assets you invest with them, most ETFs only cost somewhere in the 0.1 to 1 percent range. True, 1 percent may sound inconsequential in the scheme of things until you consider the impact on a portfolio over longer time frames. The U.S. Government Accountability Office did a report on 401(k) fees in 2009, and it concluded that by paying an extra percentage point in annual fees, you were shaving around 16 percent off your accumulated retirement savings over a 20-year span. Now you add in the loads (commissions) associated with a broker-sold mutual fund, and the difference in cost is even more glaring. As Warren Buffett and many other market mavens repeatedly admonish, high expenses are one of the biggest contributors to poor investment performance over time. ETFs were tailor-made to address this very concern.

But despite these very obvious structural and cost advantages, ETFs were by no means a slam dunk when they were first conceived of. In fact, the product went through a tumultuous early evolution, and it almost didn't survive.

The story of the ETF goes back to a primitive antecedent called the Index Participation Share (IPS) that debuted in 1989 on the American and Philadelphia Stock Exchanges. It was meant to be a product that would serve as a proxy for the S&P 500 Index, but its structure was flawed enough that it was eventually sued out of existence. Gary Gastineau tells us in his seminal book *The Exchange-Traded Funds Manual* that the Chicago Mercantile Exchange and the Commodity Futures Trading Commission successfully argued that these IPS vehicles were essentially a futures product and as such needed to trade on a futures exchange, which the Amex wasn't. Gastineau notes one other notable attempt, the SuperShares product launched by Leland, O'Brien, Rubinstein Associates. This product never really got off the ground because of its unexplainable structure, its high cost, and a skeptical environment in the wake of the 1987 crash that had been precipitated by the portfolio insurance fad.

But in 1993 a pair of American Stock Exchange executives finally get it right. They launch the SPDR fund that will track the performance of the S&P 500 Index at a lower cost and higher level of efficiency than that of the traditional index mutual funds that John Bogle had revolutionized in the 1970s at Vanguard. Nathan Most and Steven Bloom introduce their Spyder ETF in January 1993, and it goes on to become the granddaddy of ETFs, spawning a long line of descendants starting with the MidCap SPDRs in May 1995.

The Global Investors unit of Barclays Bank gets into the ETF game in 1996 with a set of 17 funds that will track each of the Morgan Stanley Country Index markets. For the first time investors can buy and sell entire foreign countries with a click, an ability we now take for granted. These Barclays ETFs will become known as the iShares family, still one of the largest lineups of ETFs to this day.

Within the next two years, mutual fund pioneer State Street will introduce the sector SPDRs, one for each of the nine sectors of the S&P 500. We'll also see the introduction of a Dow Jones–tracking

ETF—the DIA, or "Diamonds"—as well as QQQ NASDAQ index fund, affectionately known as the "Cubes."

Vanguard, which should have been an early adherent of the product given its super-low cost structure, passive characteristics, and transparency, doesn't get into the game until 2005 when Bogle retires. His reactionary screeds against the ETF revolution in the press serve as a sad episode in an otherwise storied career. He will eventually relent and acknowledge the utility of the exchange-traded structure, but by this time it is Barclays iShares that wears the ETF assets-under-management crown.

The growth of the industry in just the last decade is like nothing seen since the war bond craze that created the Wall Street–Main Street nexus to begin with. According to an April 2011 research report from the Financial Stability Board:

> At the end of Q3 2010, the global ETF industry had $1.2 trillion in assets under management, 85% in plain-vanilla ETFs referenced to equity indices, which is equivalent to 5% of global mutual fund assets and 2% of global equity market capitalisation. The industry has grown at an average of 40% a year over the past 10 years, which dwarfs the growth rate of both global mutual funds and equity markets (around 5% a year). Most ETFs are listed on US and European exchanges, but they provide exposure to a much more diverse range of markets (e.g., two of the three largest ETFs worldwide track emerging market indices).

At last count, there were 916 ETFs on U.S. exchanges. The original SPDR is still the heavyweight champ, weighing in at $89 billion in assets under management; by some measurements, it holds 7.5 percent of all assets in the entire ETF market. Its cousin GLD, the SPDR Gold Shares ETF, is a distant second place with $58 billion followed by Vanguard's Emerging Markets ETF with $47 billion under management. With products like these trading tens of millions of shares a day and garnering billions in net new inflows, it's safe to say that the ETF is now a permanent part of the firmament. These products have gone from being an alternative structure to gaining widespread acceptance among both self-directed investors and professional money managers in record time.

14

A Pill for Every Ill

"Hello?"

"Hi, is this Joshua M. Brown?"

"Yes, this is Josh. Who's this?"

"Josh, my name is Keith,* and I work in the sales and marketing department for ProShares. I'm calling because of a few articles you've written about some of our products."

"I don't write articles, Keith. I'm a blogger, and I write blog posts. But do go on."

"Fine, blog posts. Look, we don't think you're being fair when you say that our inverse ETFs are 'poisonous' and that the ProShares UltraShort Financials ETF is 'for crackheads only.' You can't call our SKF fund a crackhead, Josh."

---

* His name might have been Kevin or Keith or something like that; I don't remember. But this phone call actually did take place in the summer of 2009.

"I hear ya, but SKF *is* a crackhead fund. It was built *for* crackheads and is traded primarily *by* crackheads. Dude, you built a leveraged fund that gives people two times the exposure of the bank stocks' downside, and you released it during the worst banking crisis in modern history. Keep it real, partner. Just *own* it."

"Well, I also think there's a lot of misinformation being spread on the Internet about how our leveraged ETFs work or don't work. On an intraday basis there is very little tracking error. The negative compounding that all you bloggers are complaining about really only happens over longer periods of time,"

"OK, Keith, so what you're saying is that your leveraged funds are really only suitable for people who want a volatile trade with double the intraday move of the index itself, right?"

"Well, yes, Josh, they do work more efficiently for intraday trades and shorter holding periods, that's correct."

"Great, so we agree. Your leveraged ETFs are for crackheads. The record-breaking volatility we're already coping with right now just isn't enough for them, they need SKF and QID and such for an even *higher* high . . . like crackheads. So I'm gonna write whatever I want, Keith. Anything else I can do for you?"

(Click)

Sometimes it seems as though there are more ETFs on the market than there are stars in the sky. There are an estimated 1,335 exchange-traded products available in the global marketplace from 50 different issuers. We are still very much in the gold rush phase of the ETF revolution, with 156 brand-new funds having made their debut in just the first six months of 2011.

Every single conceivable index, sector, asset class, investment style, and classification that can have an ETF probably does at this point, and in many cases there is multiple choice. If you're looking for a way to play Chinese small-cap footwear retailers whose CEOs were born in April, there's probably an ETF for that.

In addition to the near-unlimited choices of equity ETFs, there are also a myriad of fixed-income offerings. These bond ETFs finished 2010 with over $130 billion in assets and offer investors as many segmented flavors as there are in the open-end bond fund world, including corporates, municipals by state, high yields, emerging markets, government bonds, and even a fund that lets you short government bonds. As investors went on the hunt for yield in the 2009–2011 period of ultralow rates, they poured money into these newer fixed-income products at a torrid pace. In an August 2010 research report from State Street Global Advisors, we are told that:

> *The growth of fixed-income ETF assets, which increased 78 percent in 2009, remained a key trend during the first half of the year. Fixed-income ETF assets increased by $21.2 billion or 21 percent in the six months to June 30, 2010, as the number of bond ETFs available to investors reached 105. This growth illustrates the rapid evolution in the ETF industry in order to meet the needs of investors. In 2006, just six fixed-income ETFs existed, representing approximately $20 billion in assets. In the first half of 2010, six of the 10 ETFs with the highest net cash flows were bond ETFs.*

There is perhaps no better example of the "build it and they will come" concept than what we are seeing in the bond ETF bonanza. Products and even whole new index categories are being conceived of, innovated, created, marketed, and adopted by investors at an astonishing pace.

Many fixed-income professionals have vocally denounced the bond ETF oeuvre as being a square peg jammed into a round hole. One of the big hurdles to creating and maintaining a bond index ETF is the fact that many of the smaller, more obscure bond issues that make up the index are in finite supply; hence the underlying bonds cannot actually be purchased by the fund. The Vanguards of the world have found a clever way around that by building their "index" ETF creation units using only 10 percent of the index's actual bond holdings. While they have been able to mirror just enough of the index to make their products a viable proxy, concerns continue to linger.

There has also been some consternation about mirroring the actual indexes themselves in terms of credit risk. Most mainstream bond indexes are cap-weighted, meaning the more debt a corporation issues, the larger its bonds loom in the index itself. This is a scary thought when you consider that an ETF based on this scheme could end up holding a large proportion of bonds from a heavily indebted coven of companies. Fundamentally weighted bond index ETFs have sprung up to address this concern that will stack their holdings based on creditworthiness and various debt service coverage metrics.

I'll also mention that there was a recent episode concerning a widely followed national muni bond ETF. Its price dropped precipitously on the ravings of bearish strategist Meredith Whitney when she groundlessly claimed that 50 major U.S. cities would default on their debt in the coming year. So far none have. Because muni bond professionals understood how nuanced and striated the municipal market is, very few of them even flinched as the media went into full-on sensationalism mode. But that didn't prevent a panic in the retail market as investors were dumping and even shorting the muni bond ETFs in droves. Because many municipal bonds are highly illiquid (unlike the average common stock), the market was simply unprepared for the underlying selling engendered by the sudden ETF outflows. The fund recovered once the panic subsided, but the episode illustrated that we're still in the early stages of the evolution process for bond ETFs, with a long way to go yet.

In addition to stock and bond products, several other investment categories are being addressed by the ETF revolution. We've recently seen the rise of actively managed ETFs that mirror various hedge fund styles such as long-short, convertible or merger arbitrage, distressed, global macro, and event driven. These are too new and untested to gauge their efficacy, but should they achieve their stated objectives to mirror those hedge fund index returns, you can expect a super-sexy marketing campaign aimed point blank at Mom and Pop.

Another variation gaining traction is the so-called smart index ETF, exemplified by the Wisdom Tree suite of products, which track indexes that are dividend- or equal-weighted as opposed to the traditional market cap-weighted orthodoxy.

Investors can also now access commodity-tracking exchange-traded notes (ETNs), allowing them to be short copper but long hog bellies and soybeans using these products instead of trading in the more intimidating futures market. The thing to keep in mind about an ETN is that you don't really own an equity instrument when you purchase one; you own a debt instrument (hence the word *note*). This means that your investment is only partially dependent on the particular commodity futures the fund is buying for you; it is also dependent on the solvency of the product's issuer. For example, many of these commodity ETNs have been issued by the likes of a Deutsche Bank or a UBS, depending on their ability to invest in the underlying commodity futures and to distribute those returns to holders. In addition to commodity futures–based products, a gaggle of currency ETFs beckon those who either are fed up with their incredible-shrinking-dollar risk or are looking to speculate on various outcomes in the tumultuous globalized economy.

Are we overloaded with ETFs? A reader of my blog recently sent me the fact sheet for a new fund called the Global X Fishing Industry ETF. The product describes itself thusly:

> *The Global X Fishing Industry ETF seeks to provide invest-ment results that correspond generally to the price and yield performance, before fees and expenses, of the Solactive Global Fishing Index . . . The Solactive Global Fishing Index is designed to reflect the performance of the fishing indus-try. It is comprised of selected companies globally that are engaged in commercial fishing, fish farming, fish processing or the marketing and sale of fish and fish products.*

My e-mailed response to him was "Are you f*cking kidding me?"

"A pill for every ill," he replied, and I think that about sums it up. We are, without question, completely over-ETF'd. I last counted that there were around 50 different issuers in the marketplace. That's an awful lot of people sitting around in conference rooms trying to figure out the next hot thing they can sell to us. A lot of these "innovations" are blatantly story-based at this point. Nobody ever says, "You know what my portfolio is missing? I don't have enough exposure to the aquacul-ture industry." No one ever woke up in the middle of the night worrying about whether or not they had enough exposure to beryllium prices or Brazilian hospital real estate or (fill in the needless opportunity).

But as long as we keep buying these products (by putting our dollars into them), you can rest assured that people will keep making them. Why? The fund companies get paid on the level of assets under management. If the product can make it through the first 36 months, it finally gets the all-important three-year track record, which could ultimately lead to real inflows. This ain't rocket surgery.

PART THREE

THE PITCH

I didn't know what we would be selling in the year 2000 but whatever it was we would be selling the most of it.
—Ray Kroc, founder of McDonald's

The stockbroker services his clients in the same way that Bonnie and Clyde serviced banks.
—William Bernstein

It's a proprietary strategy. I can't go into it in great detail.
—Bernie Madoff, *Barron's,* May 7, 2001

15

The Image

Look at the way most firms market themselves. The colors, themes, and stock images are always the same. Greens and browns in some cases—the rich and earthy colors that bring a bread-winning male back to his boyhood days in the forests and streams of his youth. Reds, whites, and blues—evocative of patriotism and freedom. White backgrounds denoting simplicity, gold and silver trim alerting you to the fact that inside this brochure lie treasures and a wealth of important knowledge.

The iconography of the financial advertisement also never changes. There are large wooden ships riding high and true on the "uncertain" tides of "uncertain uncertainty"—the message unmistakable: *We have persevered through squalls before, climb aboard.* There are majestic mountain ranges with snow-capped peaks the likes of which only the brave and skilled can attain. *We are your*

Sherpas, Mr. Smith. We have been to the top and can reach down to pull you up here with us.

And look, it's the cresting of a whale tail from just beneath the Pacific Ocean's briny, sun-dappled surface on the cover of this brochure. Whales are large and powerful, yet gentle and nurturing toward their young. The perfect marriage of size and compassion. *Yes, we here at Enormous Financial Supermarket Inc. have 3,000 offices and 100,000 employees around the country, but we will take care you as though you are our own offspring, Baby Beluga.*

And look! Here come the lions! The pride! The kings of the investing jungle! Running down "opportunity gazelles" on the plains of the public markets each day when the sun comes up. Regal, ferocious, not to be messed with. Masculine too, for you will never see one of those stupid female lions without the manes in a Dreyfuss ad (despite the fact that the females actually do the hunting).

The stock images used in promoting financial institutions will be familiar to you as well. They are the same ones that come in picture frames except the people are much richer looking. White sailboats dotting a smooth blue lake and old men swinging their grandchildren through the air. Septuagenarians golfing and yachting and even hiking—*there will be no all-you-can-eat Chinese buffets or coach buses in your future once you bring your assets to First American Trust Financial.* Behold the future you: You will be a man with radiantly glowing skin and a silver head of hair, smiling from ear to ear, your eyes gleaming as you carelessly put down the tennis racket and pick up an ice-cold Arnold Palmer. That twinkle in your eye? It means that you will be a gentleman with your affairs in order.

Now of course, you want that to be *you* swinging your grandchildren high above the green lawn in your tennis whites someday, right? Or leaning against that gleaming classic car you drove back in the day, now expertly restored and sitting in the driveway. These are the things you want for yourself, are they not? Well, call the 800 number then: it is all within reach.

There was a popular commercial a few years back than ran incessantly on CNBC and I'm sure on many other channels. It featured a chubby-cheeked, kind-faced gentleman giving a heartfelt toast to the bride on her wedding day, tears of joy in his eyes. And then the punch line: "But I'm just the financial advisor. Let's hear from her dad!" The Morgan Stanley logo pops up, and a thousand people across the country watching their televisions vomit in concert. My friends who work at Morgan Stanley are more likely to be deflowering the bridesmaids in a catering hall bathroom than giving wedding toasts for their clients' daughters. Again, the sentiments are sweet—*look how much our advisors care for their clients*—but give me a break.

It will be interesting to see how this old-school marketing machine will hold up in the realm of social media, where the interactions are meant to be spontaneous, two way, and without pretension. No one pays any attention to phony, soulless corporate mouthpieces on the social Web. A few brokerage firms have recently announced their pilot programs to allow their brokers to start using LinkedIn and Twitter. "Hooray!" cried the Internet! For too long social media has been sagging in the absence of a concerted big-firm marketing push. We're tired of waiting; we want those wirehouse social messages *now*. Of Morgan Stanley's 17,000 reps, about 600 of them can now use a library of pre-approved tweets that will link to the firm's "insights." In other words, Morgan Stanley will allow brokers to disseminate Morgan Stanley research and product information that has been vetted by compliance, sales, digital media, public relations, and whoever else resides along the chain of communications command. I personally can't wait to see all these "It's a Beautiful Day at Morgan Stanley" tweets all over the Web.

The truth about the efforts of these elephantine firms is that if they had their preference, all this social media and networked interaction would simply go away. They wish it would just disappear even as they take these first haltingly slow steps to show how they're embracing it. But because it won't disappear and their employees want to be treated like free human beings, the firms are forced to react to it and try to figure out a way to allow it. There are very real compliance issues involved as well as the risk that an employee could embarrass the rest of the firm, and so I can appreciate their hesitation.

It won't matter. They won't stand a chance of stopping the ebb tide of intellectual capital away from their shores. They have no shot at stemming the flow of progressive thinking that is sluicing through the streets and empowering outsiders to make their impact away from the traditional model. Social media is just one more disruptive force that is every day upending the supremacy of the bulge bracket firms. It allows thousands of smaller competitors to build their own brands and to gnaw away at the once-mighty oaks that have ruled the industry for so long. It provides evidence to the cloistered brokers inside the system that there are other ways to market and make connections besides golf tournament sponsorships and wedding toast commercials.

It's fun to chuckle at the lions and whales and wooden ships and hapless social strategies and sappy wedding tableaux in the brochures and advertisements of Wall Street. But we must also acknowledge that the trillions in assets under management with the firms that employ these tactics truly represent a triumph of marketing. The iconography never changes because it has always worked and continues to work even now. Whether it will work tomorrow remains to be seen.

16

Tales from the Sell-Side

It is the morning of June 12, 2007. My business partner Paul and I are at the NASDAQ MarketSite in New York City's Times Square sipping Jamba Juice smoothies and waiting for the festivities to begin. The event we're there for is the first annual Jamba Juice Analyst and Investor Day presentation. The newly public Jamba (JMBA) is going to trot out its slate of executives who will outline the strategic goals of the company for the first time since its backdoor public offering as a special-purpose acquisition company (SPAC).

Between Paul and me and a handful of other brokers at my firm, we are long $5 million worth of the stock for both our clients and ourselves. My personal account and my IRA are drowning in Jamba Juice stock; you could suck my portfolio up with a straw. It was an exciting retail concept with mega-expansion potential and a product that I truly loved; I was buying the stock with three hands and visiting the city's 19 Jamba locations every chance that I got. The lines were out the door that summer from Union Square to the Upper East Side, and things were looking good. The stock was selling at an all-time high that morning; it was trading around 11 bucks a share, and we had been buying it from as low as 7. There were a handful of midtier investment banks and brokerages covering the stock, most of them with price targets in the high teens. We were going to be rich.

The presentation room at NASDAQ is filled with hedge funders, shareholders, journalists, restaurant industry people, and, of course, brokerage firm analysts. The presentation began with some opening remarks from the newly appointed CEO, an ex-Burger King executive named Paul Clayton. And he is just terrible. Clayton has the personality of a bag of sand, and he kind of looks like one too. The problem is that he is supposed to be the face of a company that wants to be seen as a "healthy lifestyle brand that transcends the smoothie business." He is bald and paunchy and speaks so haltingly that I want to finish his sentences for him. My friend Paul looks at me with one of those "what the f*ck?" expressions, but I smile. "Don't worry. The vice president of product development is up next, he's going to be killer!" Paul and I walked in hoping that this presentation would result in bullish coverage from the big firms like Citi and Merrill. Clayton's so boring we're now worried that some of the existing coverage might be dropped!

Somewhere between the CFO's presentation and some remarks from Jamba's chairman, Steve Berrard (of Blockbuster Video fame), we pause for an intermission. Paul and I rush over to a window overlooking that giant five-story electronic wall display of stock quotes at the heart of the NASDAQ's headquarters. We see shares of JMBA changing hands at around $10, down 8 percent or so from the open. Paul wants to go smoke 11 cigarettes and then walk in front of a crosstown bus. I convince him to stick around for the Q&A portion of the event.

We take our seats, and the girl with the microphone tells us to raise our hands if we want to ask a question. And that's exactly the moment that I figured it all out. That's the moment I had finally gotten it through my thick head that believing Wall Street research would never, ever work for my career or my clients. I realized that it was all a giant joke and that guys like me were unknowingly delivering the punch line with every pitch.

The first question is asked by the guy from Rochdale Securities with the highest price target on The Street, 18 bucks a share. I forget the exact wording of the question, but it was something along the lines of "Why is Jamba so awesome?" If I'm not mistaken, there may have even been some light applause as he asked it among the bullish faithful in attendance. The next few questions were about the potential rollouts of new smoothie flavors or muffins or some sh*t. This nonsense goes on for an hour while the stock continues to drop; it is now under 10 according to a stolen glance at someone else's Black-Berry. Paul's face is turning pink, and I feel like a total dickhead.

And then something truly bizarre happens. One of the hottest girls I've ever seen in my life stands up and introduces herself to the room before asking her question. She is an eruption of blonde hair and self-confidence and Louis Vuitton in a room full of middle-aged, faceless male banking drones. Her name is Nicole Miller Regan, an analyst from the firm Piper Jaffray. When she begins to speak, the entire room is paying rapt attention to her every word. The only thing cuter than her face is her voice; it is at once girlish and authoritatively serious; we are in a trance, and some of us are in love. Nicole's "question" for management turns out to be more like a statement of support; she also mentions that she is "very excited" to be covering the company.

Ms. Regan had just come off a year in which she was ranked "No. 1 Stock Picker" by StarMine, related to her restaurant-sector coverage in 2005. Her buy recommendation carries weight given her track record along with the fact that Piper is the biggest firm covering the stock so far. We go back to the office willing to overlook the lackluster showing by Jamba's executives along with the weakness in the stock that day. After all, if Nicole loves it, how could anyone disagree?

Jamba will spend the next three years-and-counting breaking every investor's heart within reach. There will be a crop freeze in which the company cannot secure enough oranges later that year. Then there's a national bee shortage (I kid you not) that threatens the rest of the fruit supply chain. Next there is a hepatitis C outbreak at one of the company's storage facilities, which results in a massive recall and several customers in California being infected and hospitalized. Clayton will resign, as will almost every other executive who "presented" to us at the NASDAQ that day. Virtually all the company's hedge fund shareholders, including Paul Tudor Jones, will liquidate their holdings, crushing the stock as millions of shares are dumped relentlessly and regardless of price. Then California's entire economy falls off a cliff as every square inch of the state is foreclosed on and 12 out of 10 residents file for unemployment—kind of a bummer considering half of Jamba's stores are located there. The strategy of building company-owned stores nearly bankrupts the company, and it begins refranchising these locations at a furious pace.

The one thing that never changes as the stock trades from $11 to $0.50 a share is Piper Jaffray's buy recommendation. Piper Jaffray has a buy rating on the stock all the way down, even if Regan's commentary does get less and less "constructive" on each successive iteration. The brilliant and beautiful Nicole Miller Regan is now a managing director and senior research analyst at the firm (according to the company Web site). I have no idea how her other recommendations have done over the years, but I have her to thank for the fact that I've never listened to a brokerage firm analyst since then.

Nicole, if you're out there and reading this, congratulations on the promotion and thanks again. You may have literally saved my career.

~

There are many vestigial organs and appendages on Wall Street, but the most hilarious ones are the massive sell-side research departments of the brokerage firms.

While our appendixes and tonsils are a mere annoyance that must be removed when they act up, brokerage firm research is more like our coccyx, the remnant of a lost tail we haven't had use for in quite some time. Like these biological structures, which have lost all meaning and function through evolution, brokerage analysts are regarded with a near-universal disdain, both in the eyes of the public and within the firms themselves. They exist now primarily for the name recognition their research breeds; having analysts covering stocks has devolved into a form of brand-awareness advertising for the firms' other operations.

After decades of disappointment, the buy-side has inexorably shifted toward a preference for boutique or in-house research as opposed to the same old ambiguous ramblings from bulge bracket brokers.

For the uninitiated, the investment management business classifies itself in two different factions, the buy-side and the sell-side. The buy-side is made up of firms that manage money such as pensions, mutual funds, asset managers, and hedge funds. Buy-side analysts would be the people employed by these firms to research and analyze investments in-house. The sell-side would be the brokerage firms and investment banks that make recommendations to the buy-side in exchange for the trading commissions that come when the buy-side reacts to these calls.

According to the Bureau of Labor Statistics (BLS), there were 250,600 financial analysts employed in 2008, many of whom worked at financial institutions in New York. I can vouch for this personally; you can't swing a Yankee Stadium hot dog around without splattering mustard on one. The same BLS report found that "47% of financial analysts worked in the finance and insurance industries, including securities and commodity brokers, banks and credit institutions, and insurance carriers." The agency is forecasting 20 percent growth for the financial analyst profession over the 10 years ending 2018. This would mean the addition of 50,000 new analyst jobs for a total head count north of 300,000. I think the folks at the BLS are smoking opium with that estimate, but as we have learned, they are fortunate enough to be in a position where they can pretty much make up any stats they want. Perhaps they'll be right after all.

In Chapter 11 we discussed the Cowles Commission of the 1930s and its work that proved empirically that two-thirds of stock market forecasters had no ability to pick market-beating stocks during the five-year period he examined. Well, Cowles didn't have a $15 billion annual advertising budget, and so the research and stock rating components of the Wall Street machine outlived him and his blasted "reality." Good riddance, Cowles. We've got stocks to sell!

The presence of so many professional stock market forecasters employed at Wall Street firms is a triumph of marketing over any kind of actual mastery. We are constantly assured that brokerage firms have done their "channel checks" and their "discounted cash flow analysis modeling" on the companies they follow, but it has consistently not mattered in the aggregate. We are told that the analysts have their "boots on the ground" and their "ears to the street" in all the various metrics they watch; yet their upgrades and downgrades seem to come consistently after the fact. For these reasons, the brokerage firm analyst has steadily morphed from rock-star egghead to bought-and-paid-for grifter to oft-ignored object of ridicule in the esteem of the public.

Wall Street's analysts have always been under the microscope to some extent, as mocking the accuracy of their countless calls makes for an easily written article that readers enjoy digesting. And for researchers, the premise that Wall Street predictions are worthless in the aggregate is almost too delicious to abandon for very long. If you run a Google Scholar search, you'll find more than 500 papers on the efficacy of financial analyst research. It seems as though many academics delight in nothing more than repeatedly picking over the brokerage analyst corpse every chance they get.

There are several other ingredients in the sell-side misery stew to be aware of:

Big pools of professionally run assets (like endowments, retirement funds, and money management firms) have learned the hard way that in a bear market the brokerage firm analysts won't get them out and in a bull market their ratings are worthless as everything moves higher. After several embarrassing episodes, buy-side firms have spent more and more of their budget on internal research and analysis. Getting the early call from their broker at Goldman has never mattered less than it does in this day and age.

In addition, the hedge fund manager has become the dominant market participant of our era. Although hedge funds manage a relatively small amount of total investment dollars (somewhere above $1 trillion), their methods and tactics are the envy of the buy-side, and this includes the way they select stocks and other investments. The majority of hedge funds are paying a cut-rate 1 penny per share when they trade with the brokerage firms versus the 3 to 6 cents that most institutions used to pay. Hedge funds tend to have very little use for the research reports that brokerage firms are trying to sell them, and so why would they pay a premium execution price on their trades? As industry-standard commission rates for institutional brokerage mimic the revolution we saw in retail brokerage, it becomes very hard for the wirehouses to support a cadre of analysts that no one is listening to.

The Internet certainly hasn't helped matters either. It is upending the primacy of the Wall Street analyst just as it has with every corner of the economy it's touched since the mid-1990s. With the rise of social media and the blogosphere, opinionated experts from fields as varied as finance, health care, technology, and energy can weigh in with estimates and hypotheses of their own with virtually zero barriers to entry. A friend of mine named Leigh Drogen has started a social finance company called Estimize based on the premise that there are so many qualified (and unqualified) amateur, nonbrokerage analysts out there, that someone should be collecting and profiting from their calls as well.

With so much distrust surrounding the stock rating process, investors began adopting another type of research that completely ignored balance sheet metrics and earnings statements. As markets sped up, traders began looking for a way to cut out all the wasted time and get right to the analysis of the only thing that paid them at the end of the day: *price*. "Only price pays" became the mantra, as technical analysis became the new religion of the speculator and the hobby of the amateur.

The study of price charts is by no means new; early commodities traders had only their charts to go by back when understanding supply and demand meant the difference between eating and starving. In the canonical 1923 book *Reminiscences of a Stock Operator*, Jesse Livermore talks about charts and price throughout; there is very little discussion about the "fundamentals" of the various instruments he is speculating with.

But it wasn't until the early 2000s that technical analysis would truly reach widespread acceptance among professional and amateur traders alike. Even the stodgiest fundamentalists, schooled in the rigors of the Ben Graham school of deep value stock selection, began acknowledging that charts could help them time their buys and sells better.

This wave of acceptance for technical analysis was, in some way, a rejection of the squishier art form of listening to conference calls and meeting with company executives. There was a time when this kind of access and familiarity gave the analysts at the brokerage houses an edge that was worth something to their customers. But technical analysis stripped them of this edge, as it is entirely rooted in mathematics and pattern recognition. Anyone can look at any chart; there is no fee to be paid at the door or secret handshake required.

The big brokers have invested in technical research departments of their own over the years. Early trailblazers like Louise Yamada (Salomon Smith Barney) and Ralph Acampora (Prudential) even helped the discipline win some converts in the mainstream. But ultimately, most of these broker technical research departments have been shuttered over the years, as true approbation never quite materialized.

These days, there are as many market practitioners using technicals as there are adherents to the fundamental approach. The net result of this has been a more level playing field and yet another reason to tune Wall Street analysts out.

Between research going in-house, technicians capturing more mind share, and trading commissions shrinking to nothing, brokerage firm analysts now find themselves under siege and in danger of extinction. As we'll see shortly, once The Street is told that research cannot be used as a banking tool, budgets and jobs are cut dramatically.

The irony is that just as brokerage firm research is hitting its nadir in popularity and influence, its actual results are improving in a meaningful way! If only people were paying attention . . .

Barron's and Zacks Research do a semiannual survey of "focus lists" of the major brokerage firms. They measure how these stock picks have done versus each other and the overall market. Over the last four of these surveys, picks from the brokers have actually beaten the market on average. Even more encouragingly, for the five-year period ended December 31, 2010, the brokers' picks returned an average of 14.89 percent versus only 2.29 percent for the S&P 500. Now for many reasons, the individual investor following these picks would not have the same results. When a broker buy recommendation comes out in the premarket, the stock does not open flat with the prior night's close; it usually opens higher. The buyer of that stock on the open of trading is already behind the curve. But still it's nice to know that The Street's legions of stock pickers are a step above the old "thousand monkeys on a thousand typewriters" cliché.

Maybe.

17

Ranking for Banking

While the credibility of Wall Street's research has always been a hotly debated topic, never before had it faced a crisis of confidence like it did in the aftermath of the tech bubble's burst. This episode became the beginning of the end for the way Wall Street pimped its ratings to Corporate America in exchange for access, underwriting fees, and other assorted Scooby snacks for the bankers.

In March 2000, with the tech-laden NASDAQ trading above 5,000, a few unexpected voices of reason began to get through to us, and stocks began to top. Margin debt at both the major brokerage firms and their smaller online rivals had reached levels never before seen in market history, and so a handful of sales would beget even more selling. One day, a beloved software company called Microstrategy (MSTR) issued an earnings warning, and the stock sold off by 100 points in five minutes. That got our attention.

Bill Gates, CEO of Microsoft and the wealthiest man in the world, told reporters that technology stock prices, including his own, were wildly overvalued. Even perma-bullish Goldman Sachs strategist Abbey Joseph Cohen had begun to pull the reins in.

As thousands of strong buy-rated stocks imploded under the weight of reality during the fall of 2000, millions of investors who had taken analyst research at face value were being carried out of the markets feet first (see Figure 17.1).

The stench of losses wafted across the country like the odor of rotting flesh from a charnel house. The devastation skipped over no one; everyone's portfolio got touched. According to the *Los Angeles Times*, the stock market's crash between March 2000 and October 2002 had caused the loss of $5 trillion in public company market value. The major brokerage firms had been caught in the biggest and most destructive pay-for-play scandal in American history just as the crash in tech stocks had wrecked the nation's economy. And while there were several factors that aided and abetted this *king of all*

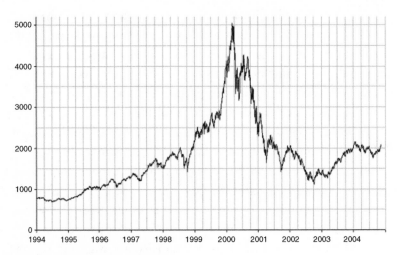

Figure 17.1 *NASDAQ 100 Index*

bubbles in technology stocks, its handmaidens at the investment banks both deserved and received the majority of the blame.

The result of this finger-pointing was the end of research as a profit center on The Street. When the Global Settlement of Conflicts of Interest between Research and Investment Banking was finally implemented on April 28, 2003, it was essentially the nail in the coffin for big bank analysts; their collective reputation would never be repaired.

The Global Settlement, as it came to be called, meant that analyst endorsements could no longer be dangled in front of a prospective banking client. It meant a separation of research from banking, thus rendering the employment of research analysts drastically less profitable.

Before we look at the effects that this watershed event had on Wall Street and its image, a bit of a history lesson is probably in order.

The game used to be played like this: "Do your initial public offering through our banking department, and our brokerage analysts will guarantee you a 'strong buy' rating for your first six months of trading." Rock-star analysts like Jack Grubman, who covered telecom for Smith Barney, would be in on the banking pitches to assure the prospective client that the company would receive a "Good Housekeeping Seal of Approval" once public. In some cases, brokerage firm analysts were even receiving banking fees, pre-IPO shares of stock, or a cut of the underwriting's profits.

In the most extreme cases, the bankers were actually dictating upgrades and downgrades directly to the firm's analysts based on how much banking business a public company was doing with them.

But here's the thing: In a bull market, people overlook some of the dirty deeds being committed under the surface. Everybody's making money, and so who cares if the research on Wall Street is compromised? All manner of sins are either excused or ignored so long as the music keeps playing and people still feel like dancing. Investors had been dancing for almost two decades while brokerage firms had been secretly diluting the integrity of their research in the name of bigger profits.

A July 2000 article from the *Knowledge@Wharton* magazine collected a handful of academic studies illustrating this slide in propriety. The word was getting out, and the jig was almost up. A finance professor at Dartmouth named Kent L. Womack noted that analysts in the early 1990s were making roughly six "buy" recommendations for every one "sell" call on the stocks they covered. But by the year 2000, that ratio had exploded to something closer to 50 buys to every sell rating. Another study found that analysts who had brought in underwriting business to their firms could be paid "bonuses that are two to four times those of analysts without underwriting contributions."

In July 2001, the acting chairperson of the SEC, Laura Unger, testified before the House of Representatives Subcommittee on Capital Markets, Insurance, and Government Sponsored Enterprises. You should have been there, it was hilarious. But seriously, the findings in her report were so off the wall that even people with no understanding of the regulations were blown away by the brazen immorality of it all. In the eyes of the ordinary citizen, Wall Street's behavior in this era was the business-world equivalent of slapping babies and stepping on puppy dogs.

Here were some of the items that Unger laid bare for all to see on Capitol Hill that day:

> *The lines between research and investment banking have indeed blurred. Seven of the nine firms inspected reported that investment banking had input into analysts' bonuses and the analyst hiring process. At at least one of those firms, 90 percent of an analyst's bonus is based on investment banking revenue.*

The staff inspections found that investment banking did not formally supervise analysts. However, analysts assist investment banking by consulting on IPOs, mergers and acquisitions, participating in pre-IPO roadshows, and initiating research of prospective investment banking clients. Interviews with former analysts revealed that it was well understood by all of these analysts that they were not permitted to issue negative opinions about investment banking clients.

About one quarter of the analysts inspected own securities in companies they cover. The staff found that 16 of 57 analysts reviewed made 39 investments in a company they later covered. All of the investments were pre-IPO. Most significantly, examiners found that three of these analysts traded contrary to their research report recommendations.

Examiners also found that in 26 of 97 lock-ups reviewed, research analysts may have issued "booster-shot" research reports. These reports reiterated "buy" recommendations shortly before, or just after, the expiration of the "lock-up" period. ("Lock-ups" are the time period preventing insiders and others obtaining pre-IPO shares from selling the shares.) In each of these instances, the firm underwrote the IPO, or the firm's analysts owned stock in the company.

These findings had come from on-site examinations of the nine largest investment banks and brokerages of the era. It was a "you gotta be kidding me" moment for both investors and lawmakers.

There was always a sense that Wall Street research was a little bit biased, but nobody had any idea to what extent. Now they knew.

The mustachioed Frank Quattrone, a Silicon Valley deal maker working for Credit Suisse, became emblematic of these shenanigans. Quattrone had become legendary for having shepherded the IPOs of such bubble-era darlings as Netscape and Amazon.com. He had famously made $100 million in a single year at the height of the IPO boom. But between his "Friends of Frank" IPO-hoarding program, his directives to employees to "clean out those e-mail inboxes," and other unsavory machinations, he became Public Enemy No. 1 in the eyes of the regulators. He was tried in 2003 for obstruction of justice, and the jury was hung. A later trial resulted in his conviction and sentencing to a term of up to 20 years in prison. But this was eventually overturned in a federal appeals court, as was the lifetime ban from the securities industry. Long story short, the man who turned brokerage research into a tool of bribery and brazenly conned the entire investing public had fought the government to a standstill, and by 2006 a judge in New York had dropped all charges against him.

His story should serve as a cautionary tale about believing what any banking firm has to say about the stocks it is rating.

But there would be an even greater scandal that would forever alter the way the public looked at Wall Street equity research. I am referring, of course, to the story of Henry Blodget, the Merrill Lynch analyst whose conscience got the better of him in the midst of the maelstrom. Blodget put his reservations about the ratings he was slapping on Web stocks into an e-mail to his higher-ups. But despite his misgivings, Henry continued to play the game. His conscience was apparently subservient to his desire to keep his job, as later e-mails will show. And who could blame him? He was young and ambitious, climbing high in the world of finance. He didn't possess the frame of reference or experience to truly understand how badly it would all end.

In the trail of e-mails that then–New York State attorney general Eliot Spitzer would famously use against Blodget, the ginger-complexioned boy wonder of Internet analysis can be seen encouraging his fellow Internet analysts at Merrill Lynch to keep the balls in the air. This despite his tacit acknowledgment in June 2000 that "this thing is a powder keg" and that several of his buy-rated holdings were "dogs" and "pieces of sh*t."

In one illustrative example of what most of The Street's analysts were up to those days, Blodget names Internet Capital Group (ICGE) to Merrill's Top Ten Technology Stocks list on September 12, 2000. ICGE was a "dot-com incubator," meaning it had no business other than allocating capital to other Internet companies that had no businesses themselves. It sounds hilarious in hindsight, but companies like these had raised billions in the public markets by simply showing up. But the NASDAQ had already topped six months prior, and anyone with any sense had been selling these types of bullsh*t companies with both hands. A month after naming ICGE to his top 10 list, Blodget responded to an e-mailed inquiry about the company like this:

> No helpful news to relate [regarding ICGE], I'm afraid.
> This has been a disaster, there really is no floor to the stock.

Unfortunately for Merrill's retail clients, this particular opinion of Henry's never made it into one of his "research" reports.

What Merrill and the other 10 largest investment banks had decided, subconsciously or not, was that their banking clients were more lucrative than their retail brokerage clients. A 10 percent fee for doing a billion-dollar Internet company IPO is worth $100 million to the bank. Retail buy and sell transactions on that company's stock would never even come close, especially in terms of profitability.

Essentially, the brokerage firms that spent billions advertising how trustworthy they were had decided that Mom and Pop could go f**k themselves. I could rephrase that, but why bother; this was a black-and-white betrayal with the most vulnerable investors as the biggest victims.

As the NASDAQ began its mind-blowing nosedive from 5,100 down to an eventual cratering of around 1,000 or so, investors had been wiped out. Companies like eToys and Pets.com, having just raised billions from the investing public, were going out of business in a matter of months. Stockbrokers stopped returning calls, and all those high-flying neophyte traders online had turned their Bar Mitzvah money into a pile of smoldering ashes. The people were angry, and they wanted blood. They wanted heads to roll down Wall Street, and one man was early enough to the opportunity to give this to them, making his own career in the process.

Eliot Spitzer had already been the scourge of Wall Street before the dot-com mania was in full swing. As a liberal-leaning prosecutor and attorney general, he had already made it clear that he was no pushover for the banking interests of New York State. Spitzer's eyes were on the governorship and eventually the White House. The chance to wage a high-profile crusade against the banking bad guys was like a big, fat, juicy fastball right down the middle of the plate. Spitzer would knock that ball out of the park and become the face of the public's wrath, the *people's champion*.

Henry Blodget's e-mail trail combined with his near-celebrity status and position at America's largest brokerage firm made him an easy target for Spitzer. He had become the flashpoint of the controversy even though there were thousands of bankers and analysts who were in on the scam. His e-mails would become incontrovertible evidence that The Street had been using its research as a means to do more banking while allowing its millions of brokerage clients to twist in the wind.

Blodget certainly didn't deserve to receive as much of the personal scorn as was heaped upon him, but once he became the focal point, there was no escape. Things would turn out OK for him in the end. While settling financially (a $2 million penalty and a $2 million disgorgement), he also accepted a securities industry bar. Years later, he would start up a successful digital media property called *The Business Insider*, a blog network I occasionally contribute to. These days, he can be seen traipsing around the World Economic Forum in Davos, Switzerland, wearing a fur hat and a Cheshire grin. He is a smart guy and surely knows deep down that being bounced from a career in Wall Street research is the best thing that's ever happened to him.

As for Eliot Spitzer, his historic victory over Wall Street made him a shoo-in for the governorship of New York. Shortly after his coronation as National Good Guy, we got a glimpse of his, shall we say, less altruistic side. With tactics like using the state troopers as his own Imperial Guard and personal spy ring, he lost much of the goodwill that the Global Settlement had earned him just a few years earlier. His inability to masturbate was his eventual undoing, as the trafficking of a prostitute across state lines would force him to resign his elected office shortly afterward. Elliott ended up landing a nightly talk show on CNN called *In the Arena*, but it didn't last very long, perhaps owing to the former governor's excess of likability.

In the end, Eliot Spitzer and Henry Blodget did have a chance for a public reconciliation during an Internet video interview that served as a touching coda to the battle that changed the nature and appearance of Wall Street research forever.

18

The Global Settlement

"Hi Doctor Ed, it's Josh. How's it going this morning?"

"You know, the usual. I have a full day of a bunch of patients coming in today. How's my stocks looking?"

"So far, so good in the premarket. There were a bunch of analyst upgrades and downgrades. Let me see . . . Oh, okay, Lehman Brothers just went to an 'overweight' rating on Intel . . ."

"Wait, a what rating?"

"Overweight. Intel."

"What the hell does that mean?"

"Not sure. I guess they're saying Intel's gotten fat, could stand to drop a few pounds."

"Come on, seriously? They like it or they don't?"

"Yeah, all the brokerage firms are too scared to say 'buy' or 'strong buy' anymore. So they all have different ways to say it now. It's all messed up, I don't know."

"Okay . . . but so 'overweight' means good?"

"Yes, they mean, like, you should be overweight Intel relative to the index's weight because it should perform better than most stocks. I think. Nobody really knows. The research reports now have three pages explaining this stuff, but it's all gibberish. I think on purpose. The firms are all freaking out. There's this massive billion-dollar settlement hanging over them. I don't even think *they* know what's going on."

"Okay, this is great, really comforting. What about Home Depot?"

"Hmmmm, good old HD. Let's have a look . . . OK, Prudential just raised it to a 'strong neutral'"

"Alright Josh, I've heard enough. Call me when they go back to 'buys' and 'sells.'"

~

The aspect of the Global Settlement that got the most attention in the media was that dollar figure—a billion dollars. It seemed like so much money then; now it's a rounding error in an age where the government has run up a $14.5 trillion national debt. We have banks in this world that write off a billion dollars a month in bad mortgage debt. We have hedge fund managers that make billions of dollars plural for a year's work. Social network Facebook is currently valued at around $100 billion, and it has like 25 employees. A billion dollars has become a laughably silly amount, an anachronistic Dr. Evil punch line.

But back then, it was the real deal. It signaled that the bullsh*t was over and that there would be a real reckoning for the research-and-banking scandal. A triumphant press release from the National Association of Securities Dealers (NASD, now FINRA) announced the terms:

> On April 28, 2003, NASD, the U.S. Securities and Exchange Commission (SEC), the New York Stock Exchange (NYSE), the National Association of State Securities Administrators [sic] (NASAA), and the New York State Attorney General announced the final terms of the Global Settlement of Conflicts of Interest between Research and Investment Banking (Global Settlement).

> The Global Settlement followed joint investigations by the regulators into alleged conflicts of interest between investment banking and securities research at brokerage firms.

> As a result of the investigation, ten of the nation's top investment firms agreed to pay $1.4 billion—$387.5 million of it in restitution to be returned to harmed investors through a process overseen by the SEC, and $487.5 million in penalties. Funds have also been earmarked for investor education and to help pay for independent research for investors. The firms have also agreed to reforms in the way they do business to help prevent these conflicts in the future.

Of course, in the context of the credit crisis that occurred just four years later, we now know that this settlement meant absolutely nothing and didn't prevent a thing. The debacle that would follow it and plunge the entire world into disarray involved even more dangerous and disgraceful conflicts throughout the banking industry. But at the time, the Global Settlement was seen as serious business.

Wall Street executives even managed to look and act suitably penitent for a time. They gave the appearance that they were cleaning up their act, the way children do after coming out of a time-out. The banking and brokerage colossus Citigroup even ousted its own architect, Sandy Weill, and put a schmucky lawyer named Chuck Prince in charge just to stay on Spitzer's good side.

Fortunately for the Masters of the Universe, the next blood orgy of debt and destruction was lurking just around the corner in the credit and real estate markets. But for now, the bankers and brokers were cowed and under control.

The Global Settlement was about more than just the money (which was actually $1.5 billion if you're keeping score). It was about a commitment to investor education and the distribution of third-party independent research alongside the firm's own research for each stock report.

My friend and fellow financial blogger Tom Brakke had an important role in the aftermath of the settlement's decree. Tom is the president of TJB Research, an investment firm consultancy. He recently wrote about his experiences with the settlement for *CFA Magazine*:

> *The Global Research Analyst Settlement, one of the biggest regulatory actions in financial market history, was born of conflicts of interest . . . Twelve investment banks entered into the settlement, for an advertised price tag of US$1.5 billion (plus significant implementation costs). Its terms included*

mandated changes in operations, the funding of investor
education and restitution, and the provision of indepen-
dent, third-party research to clients of the firms. My role as
a consultant was running an independent research program
on an arm's-length basis for one of the settling firms.

Tom notes that the process of interpretation and implementation
of the settlement's various dictates was hampered by the adversarial
relationship between the two sides. The brokerage firms were willing
to settle, but were not willing to be steamrolled, to borrow a favorite
term of Mr. Spitzer.

With hundreds of millions of dollars up for grabs in the independent research space, vendors came out of the woodwork. Tom's job
was to design a process by which research providers could be chosen
in such a way that the settlement's terms were satisfied.

As to how the "investor education" money was spent, I have no
idea. Maybe it was used to fund the creation of some kind of furry
mascot, like Dewey the Due Diligence Dog. And maybe it was used to
bring Dewey around to public schools to teach kids about price-to-
earnings ratios or something; I don't know. It's not worth researching and writing about because I'm sure it was money wasted; nobody
learned anything.

I can also tell you that investors had very little interest in the
third-party, independent research reports that firms were now
dumping on them. The reports were mostly generic, produced by
a software program with no real opinion or sexiness or insight.
Millions of reports that were just algorithmic number or letter
grades. I had access to all of it, and I would print it out for mailings
just to keep my compliance officer from having a panic attack. In
fact, I think the biggest impact that all that third-party research

had was on the environment—brokerage firms were felling twice the amount of trees than usual every time they sent a buy recommendation out to a client.

My cynical take is that both of these initiatives, the research and the education, were well meaning but probably haven't amounted to much for investors.

How were the brokerages impacted?

A *BusinessWeek* article from 2002 captures the insanity of coming up with new ways to rate stocks. Journalist Jane Black comes away from her discrete discussions with analysts both puzzled and a bit amused. There is a sense of an "Alice in Wonderland" environment at the major firms as they seek to invent new terminology that will both convey an opinion and yet be vague enough that no one actually calls them on anything.

> *Some analysts argue that any new system should have just two ratings: buy and sell. "After all, that's all you can do with a stock," quips one analyst. "You can't market perform it."*

The nonsensical "underweights" and "market performs" that evolved from this process are still with us. Fortunately, the majority of analyst calls are no longer heeded anyway; they serve as fodder for new headlines on the financial Web, and that's about all.

Business returned to normal between the research and banking divisions of the firms involved over the years since the settlement was implemented. The firms claim that there's a "Chinese Wall" betwixt the two factions and that the compensation stuff has all been cleaned up, but there is still an understanding that you don't downgrade the big clients of the firm.

When analysts do downgrade stocks, in my experience, it tends to come only after a slew of weak earnings reports and in the context of a stock price that has already been falling for months. In fact, ask most experienced traders about which type of sell-side call gets them most excited and they'll almost unanimously answer that they love when a broker goes negative. The value investors will wholeheartedly agree.

It turns out that a great number of market participants these days have made it a habit to fade the calls of the brokerage firm analyst, even as these calls grow fainter and less effective with every passing quarter.

19

Storytime

The most effective method of selling anything in this world is through storytelling. The holy books of all the world's major religions employ this very tactic. So do the best commercials, lawyers, and universities. "Our product will change your life . . . ," "Ladies and gentlemen of the jury . . . ," "Our students go on to achieve success beyond their wildest dreams . . ."

But try as they might, none of them even come close to matching the storytelling ability of Wall Street.

The selling of financial products and services has evolved into an art form all its own, dating from The Street's humble beginnings as a hub for professional speculators. When civilian money became a more important part of the daily doings on Wall Street, it became necessary to develop a story component in order to direct that money to where it was needed. As we learned in Chapter 2, the very first story that brought

Main Street to the table involved fighting fascists with U.S. war bonds. This was a very straightforward story to tell, and there was a tinge of patriotism involved that made it so that the bonds really sold themselves. But as the investment firms grew larger and the products grew in sophistication, so too did the stories themselves out of necessity.

And it is not just product that needs to be sold. Strategies have received their own stories as well. "Buy and hold" is one of the greatest stories ever told, this despite the fact that in the past century we've seen 25 cyclical bear markets and two bone-crushing secular bear markets. Had you bought and held equities in the late 1920s, you would not have been back to breakeven until the early 1950s. A basket of stocks bought in 1966 would have been worth the same nominal dollar amount 16 years later in 1982. But buy and hold means captive pools of assets to assess steady fees from, and so buy and hold is ingrained in the Wall Street sales pitch to America. The stories illustrating the futility of "trying to time the markets" have taken on the canonical general acceptance of an Aesop fable over the years. Soccer moms and grade school children will tell you that you shouldn't look a gift horse in the mouth, step on a sidewalk crack, walk beneath a ladder, or try to time the market. Whether they've tried or not isn't the point (most of them haven't). This message has been steadily drilled into their heads by the marketing machine for so long that it has become almost law. Unfortunately for the buy-and-hold faithful, we now find ourselves experiencing the so-called hundred-years storm about every seven years these days.

How good is Wall Street at crop-dusting America with these types of stories and syllogisms? Picture Hans Christian Anderson himself putting his grandchildren to sleep around a campfire with a Brothers Grimm volume of fairy tales. Then you *might* have a sense of the artfulness and narrative dexterity we're talking about.

Now keep in mind that we're not talking about trickery per se, but storytelling as a means to coax investment dollars into a given theme or thesis, often with the investors' best interest in mind. And while the intentions of the storytellers may be good, they certainly do not excuse the carnival-barker nature of it all. In my relatively short time on The Street, I've seen hundreds of billions of dollar thrown in all kinds of erratic directions in pursuit of story. The reason it continues to this day is very simple: it works. It moves units, generates commissions, and raises assets. People love stories, and they react to them frequently.

The need for a narrative or metaphorical connection is as old as the human race itself. The Neolithic cave paintings found across Western Europe are one of the earliest examples of the storytelling tradition and its intertwined relationship with survival itself. The paintings tell of how the clan is fed and nourished on the animals it hunts; this is an instruction manual in story form using the very earliest written language—pictures.

To a large extent, the human mind is hardwired for story; it is the primary way in which we understand the world and pass on what we've learned to future generations. And not any story will resonate; there are very specific story structures that affect us all in a primal way. It is no coincidence that in every part of the world, there is some significant and revered version of one of the following seven story arcs or plots:

1. Overcoming the monster

2. Rags to riches

3. The quest

4. Voyage and return

5. Comedy

6. Tragedy

7. Rebirth or transformation

Examples of each of these seven arcs had been independently developed by ancient cultures with absolutely no contact with one another whatsoever. This doesn't happen by accident.

Christopher Booker spent 30 years researching his seminal 2005 book on the subject, *The Seven Basic Plots*. The psychoanalyst Carl Jung took a shot at this idea, calling these archetypal stories the "development and integration of the mature self." Joseph Campbell has also written some landmark treatises on the subject, his dissection of the classic hero myth types ultimately inspiring George Lucas to combine them all into the story for the Star Wars movies.

And without even trying, you can see how adroitly these seven basic story types have been adapted by the investment industry in order to market and sell product: *Overcoming the monster* with inflation-proof bonds, portfolio insurance, and principal-protected index funds. The *rags to riches* promises of being in on the penny stock that explodes by 1,000 percent or investing in the newest category of hot growth funds. A *voyage* to the emerging market stocks and bonds that simply must be a part of every portfolio. The *rebirth* of a corporate turnaround stock and the *transformational* opportunities to be exploited in the technology sector.

Wall Street is extraordinarily adept at selling through story, and when no story is immediately apparent, it will create one out of thin air. Themes sell funds and stocks and strategies. Themes get people to pay attention to television appearances and newsletters. They get investors talking to each other, which sells even more stuff. Themes are the alpha and the omega of Wall Street's very existence; they are the hook that pulls in the Main Street money no matter how many of them have been total busts. The same investors who chased Y2K software stocks through the nonevent of 1999's turn to 2000 were the same who, only three years later, were piling into post-9/11 security stocks like Taser International.

But when it comes to thematic investing, most of the money is made by those who germinate the very concept itself, positioning early and then spinning the yarn while encouraging its dissemination. This is a specialty of brokerage firms and investment banks, and the fund industry is also no slouch.

One could go year by year and pick out a different fad or theme that had captured the attention and dollars of the investor class. In fact, I've done just that in Table 19.1.

Table 19.1 *A Snapshot of Fads and Themes, 1996–2010*

Year	Investing Fads and Themes	As Personified By
1996	Initial Public Offerings, Microbrews, Irrational Exuberance	Alan Greenspan, Federal Reserve Chairman
1997	Viagra, Cigars, Telecom/Cable	John Malone, Chairman of Liberty Media
1998	E-tail, Venture Capital, Clicks & Mortar	Jeff Bezos, Founder and CEO of Amazon.com
1999	B2B Internet, Y2K, Tracking-Stocks, Carve-Outs	Frank Quattrone, Silicon Valley Investment Banker
2000	Wireless, Optical Networking, Competitive Local Exchange Carriers	Jack Grubman, Smith Barney Telecom Analyst
2001	Old Economy, Defensive Stocks	Warren Buffett, Legendary Value Investor
2002	Security Tech and Defense Companies	Donald Rumsfeld, Secretary of Defense
2003	Biotech, Fiber To The Premises, More Biotech	Mark B. McClellan, FDA Commissioner
2004	VoIP, 3G Wireless Rollout, China	Patricia Russo, CEO of Lucent Technologies
2005	Oil, Homebuilders, India, Viaticals/Life Settlements	T Boone Pickens, Oil & Gas Magnate

(*continued*)

Table 19.1 (*continued*)

Year	Investing Fads and Themes	As Personified By
2006	Residential Real Estate, Green/ Cleantech, LBOs, Video Games	Bob and Bruce Toll, Home Builders
2007	Private Equity, Hedge Funds, BRIC, Commercial RE	Stephen Schwartzman, CEO of Blackstone Group
2008	Gold, Leveraged ETFs, Short-selling	John Paulson, Hedge Fund Manager
2009	Dollar Carry Trade, Emerging Markets, Commodities	Benjamin Bernanke, Federal Reserve Chairman
2010	Mobile Web, Metals and Miners, Tablets/Smartphones, Venture Capital	Steve Jobs, Apple CEO
2011	Social Media IPOs, Currency Trading, Risk-On Risk-Off, Dividends	Angela Merkel, Chancellor of Germany

Each of the fads and themes in the table had specific stocks, funds, and strategies attached to them. Between wholesalers getting the word out to the brokerage sales forces and the traditional power of blanket advertising, all of them were immensely lucrative to The Street and its denizens.

But story is not inherently evil. In fact, it can be quite helpful for investors looking to understand secular bull markets and boom-lets in various sectors that they may not have thought much about before. One example of a story that panned out would be the coining of the term *BRIC*. In 2001, Goldman Sachs economist Jim O'Neill made the single biggest, most profitable call of the decade to come. In his team's landmark Global Economics Paper #66, also called "Building Better Global Economic BRICs," he invented the term *BRIC*, which stands for Brazil, Russia, India, and China as an invest-ment theme. Like most big macro themes, demographics were the central premise of why these four nations would be deserving of our investment dollars. O'Neill's story was that the capitalist constructs of these four nations were developing just as their homegrown middle-class populations were exploding.

From his paper, we learned that:

> *Over the next 50 years, Brazil, Russia, India and China—the BRICs economies—could become a much larger force in the world economy. Using the latest demographic projections and a model of capital accumulation and productivity growth, we map out GDP growth, income per capita and currency movements in the BRICs economies until 2050 . . . The results are startling. If things go right, in less than 40 years, the BRICs economies together could be larger than the G6 in US dollar terms. By 2025 they could account for over half the size of the G6. Currently they are worth less than 15%. Of the current G6, only the US and Japan may be among the six largest economies in US dollar terms in 2050.*

This combination of rapid gentrification, sudden internal demand for goods and services, and large-scale infrastructure build-out made the BRIC story irresistible. A thousand ADRs and funds of all types were created here in the states to satiate investor demand as the story got out. And you know what? It worked.

Trillions in wealth were created as the world-changing shifts that this paper predicted came to pass. China has since surpassed all the nations in Europe and Japan to become the second largest economy in the world. The stock markets of Brazil, India, and Russia have since doubled and then doubled again. Had you allowed O'Neill's research to tuck you in and tell you this particular bedtime story, you'd have made more money this past decade than by doing virtually anything else conceivable.

Investors who latched on to this concept made a fortune during an era of flat performance for most developed markets and got in early on a megatrend that looks to remain in force for some time to come.

But sometimes when a story works, it works so well that the imitators burst onto the scene at exactly the wrong moment. Sometimes there is so much money in a trade that there is literally no one left to come in and buy. A good case in point might be the precious metals infatuation that had reached its boiling point by the spring of 2011. By 2010, gold had been outperforming virtually every other asset class on the menu for a decade. As it became apparent to ordinary investors that central banks around the world were in a "currency race to zero," protecting themselves from inflation led millions of people into the various gold and gold miner funds.

With this rush into gold, some of the yellow metal's more rambunctious cousins like silver and platinum began making parabolic moves higher. The Street seized this opportunity and began pumping out investment products tied to the prices of various metals futures and mining opportunities. The mouthpieces of funds with picture-perfect names like Midas and Physical Currency began extolling the ineluctable virtues of hard assets everywhere you looked. By the end of 2010, silver was up 80 percent for the year, while the even more speculative palladium had run 96 percent (versus a more modest 27 percent return for gold). Articles about kids putting their savings into silver to pay for their college tuition began appearing. We also began seeing the inevitable cartoonish product launches of products like the Physical White Metals Basket Shares ETF on December 1 of that year. It was designed to give investors exposure to silver, platinum, and palladium. I remember sarcastically saying to myself, "Terrific, they're now classifying these things by color, this will end well." It didn't; by the following spring, once Mr. Market was certain that everyone was in, silver plummeted after briefly touching its early 1980s nominal highs of $50 an ounce. A good story gone bad, with no shortage of adherents now trapped with losing positions and hoping for a happy ending, someday.

And lest I paint a picture of a simple one-way con, keep in mind that in almost all cases The Street was itself taken in by the stories it was telling. Some of the heaviest casualties of the dot-com bust were felt in the mutual fund complex, including the decimation of Wharton-educated professional stewards of capital from coast to coast. But perhaps an even more telling example would be the buying and selling of toxic mortgage bonds among the banks themselves, each major investment house a counterparty to all the rest while they circulated each other's weapons-grade plutonium paper. The extent to which Citigroup, Lehman Brothers, Merrill Lynch, and Bear Stearns got high on their own supply was absolutely epic. These were the best and brightest, and they had become intoxicated on their own bullsh*t right up until the very end. The banks found themselves not only selling the "housing as a never-ending rally" story; they became the biggest buyers and believers of the story as well. This was thematic investing turned fatal.

Sometimes a story is so powerful that even the teller forgets that it began as a way to sell stuff.

20

The Straight Line

And now, for the first time ever, the Straight-Line Pitch (also known as the Lehman Method) is in print.

What you are about to read is the infamous but never-before-published script that's sold thousands of stock ideas and opened millions of retail brokerage accounts over the last 50 years. It has hundreds of authors; it had been reshaped and reworked by several generations before it reached my desk in the 1990s. At its core, it has changed remarkably little considering it has faced the dawn of the information age with the advent of computers and the Internet. Its use continues even now in the era of wireless phones, text messaging, e-mail, and all the other innovations that have changed the world over the decades. The brokers say that pitching new investors is "a numbers game." One out of ten qualified investors will open a new account when a broker uses this pitch—then and now—so why should it *have to* change?

I wrestled for a while with the decision of being the first person to publish something that has been so clandestine and fundamental to the brokerage business for so long. Then I came to the conclusion that someone had to do it and it may as well be me. Right now there are 4,500 brokerage firms in the United States with roughly 163,000 branch offices and more than 630,000 registered reps. Excluding the dually registered advisors, the brokers who work in bank branches, and those who serve institutional investors, these reps are likely using some variation of the Straight Line Pitch even if they don't realize it. You know the lines . . .

> "Stretch with me this one time, and I'll never have to ask you to stretch ever again."
>
> "You'll be smiling from ear to ear."
>
> "You'll be laughing all the way to the bank."
>
> "This trade will be the cornerstone of a 20-year relationship."
>
> "This will be the best decision you've made all year."
>
> "The only problem you'll have is that you didn't know me well enough to buy more."
>
> "Let the results convince you that you've made the right decision."
>
> "Let me take you under my wing, and I have a funny feeling that some of your other accounts will find a home here with me as well."

The Straight Line is impulse selling at its most aggressive, and there have been hundreds of thousands schooled and steeped in its traditions over the years. Since its beginnings in the Water Street and Madison Avenue branches of Shearson Lehman, the Straight Line has been taught and retaught a million times during countless boardroom meetings and brokerage firm training sessions. Like most potent weapons, some have used this pitch for good and some for evil. It has been used to begin relationships between dedicated brokers and clients that have lasted decades. It has also been used by churn artists and those selling over-the-counter "house stocks" complete with fraudulent markups built into the prices. Just as nuclear power can be used to heat homes or to make whole cities disappear, so too can the Straight Line connect an investor with both good brokers and bad ones.

With the mass migration toward the more holistic and client-focused investment advisory model, those who had initially built their businesses on selling product have since dropped this pitch from their repertoire. There is still, however, a small core of brokers who are consistently "cracking new accounts" using this method. But these days, the vast majority of new clients they're bringing in with this old-school rap are in some of the most remote areas of the country. It's not that the rural folks have any less common sense than their more cosmopolitan counterparts on whom this doesn't work anymore; it's just that they've heard it less and so are still susceptible.

Almost anyone who's ever gotten a cold call from a broker can jokingly recite snippets of this pitch. Its phrases and topics and lines come from a host of different selling books, Shafiroff's included, but they've been molded and modified and stripped down and embellished over the years based on that original framework. No one's ever seen the whole thing in print before, the way it's been handed down from broker to broker. Until now.

Before we get into the specific closes and rebuttals of the pitch, I'll first lay out the methodology and the structure of the Straight Line. The way it's been taught traditionally is as follows:

Picture yourself chasing a prospective customer down a hallway (I kid you not; this is how it's explained). All along the hallway are doors on each side. Each of these doors is an excuse for why the prospect can't buy the stock today—no money, no time to talk, can't decide without doing his own research, needs to consult a wife or business partner, etc. At the very end of the hall is the only door you want him to go through—the "yes" door. Your job is to chase the prospect down the hallway during the course of the call and slam each of those "excuse" doors shut as he attempts to escape through them.

Each time a prospect makes an excuse for why he can't buy, the broker using the straight line is to use one of four rebuttals to put that argument to bed. When the prospect switches his reason for not being able to buy, he has invalidated both of these excuses and any that come after it; at this point the broker has the prospect "on the run."

As sickening as this all is, there is some logic to it. Imagine you call a friend to go to the movies with you, and he tells you he has to be somewhere at 6 p.m. so he can't. Now imagine that you rebut that excuse by informing him the movie is only 87 minutes long, which leaves him plenty of time. If he then says that he can't go because he isn't feeling well, he has just put himself on the run; all his reasons for not being able to go are lies, and it is up to you to discover the "real" reason. By the same token, when a prospect first says he can't buy a stock because he isn't liquid enough and then says he can only buy if he has some time to do some homework, he is telling you that neither reason is the real one in terms of why he isn't buying.

The well-trained broker is actually thrilled to hear the prospect make these excuses, especially when the prospect dances from one to the next. Each door slammed shut brings the prospect closer to either hanging up or agreeing to the trade. Brokers are armed with enough ammunition to never have to hang up before the prospect relents or clicks the phone down. The conversation may veer off into many different directions, but the broker is trained to bring it back onto the path toward a close, the origin of the Straight Line's nomenclature. The structure is as follows:

> *The introduction:* "Hi Bill, this is Alex Stevenson from Rocky & Bullwinkle Securities. How are you? Great to hear!"

Notice how the broker addresses the prospect by his first name. This is to engender a sense of familiarity over the phone. The broker is also informing you that he is on your level, a peer, and not one of your employees who calls you Mr. Smith.

> *Introduction continued:* "You were recently contacted by a member of my staff in reference to the stock market. At the time we promised only to contact you with a trading idea that we felt had truly explosive potential. If you have a pen handy, I'd like to give you the ticker symbol and have you take down some brief notes. Let me know when you're ready . . ."

The trap is baited. If there is resistance at this point, the broker will throw out an example of the last idea he was bringing to investors that doubled or tripled in value. Keep in mind that these lines are delivered with a gargantuan amount of conviction and sincerity. On paper they hardly compare to what they sound like when delivered by tough-sounding New York brokers oozing with confidence and market-beating bravado over the phone.

Assuming the client assents to being pitched, the broker then launches into a three-part presentation of the stock idea he is selling; let's call it Acme Bowling Ball Co. (ticker ABC):

> *Compare sells:* "Last month similar company XYZ traded from 5 to 50 based on ___!"
>
> *Fundamentals:* "Acme Bowling is earning ___ and trading at only ___ times cash flow!"

Catalyst: "Everything I've told you is already known by the pros, but wait 'til you hear this!"

By the time this catalyst is delivered; the broker has made the case for why the stock must be bought *right now.* This is followed by a few questions that were designed to get the prospect in "yes mode," like:

"Do we agree that owning undervalued companies such as Acme Bowling before everyone else discovers them is the key to making money in the market?"

At this point, the broker will close for the first time (of many). He will propose a trade to the prospect in the amount of $50,000 or $100,000 worth of ABC, "just to get the relationship started." He does not expect to get an order of this size; the purpose of asking for something so ridiculous is both to give himself room to come down on the share amount in future closes and to avoid looking like a little piker. Brokers are trained to expect a no to this first close and to relish it. "Every no gets me closer to a yes," we are all told in those godawful Zig Ziglar books.

Once the prospect says no to the trade for the first time, the actual sale has begun. The broker next gets the prospect to admit, out loud, that although he can't do the trade because of reason X, he at least agrees that the stock is going to trade higher. Once the client agrees that the trade itself is a winner, then it becomes a matter of convincing him that the trade needs to be done right now.

At this point, the broker will alternate between addressing specific objections and segueing into different "power closes," each of which ends with the broker asking for the order one more time. The broker is armed with three to five rebuttals to combat each of the typical objections he will encounter. Objections include:

- ○ "Let me call you back."
- ○ "I don't like the market right now."
- ○ "I'm not liquid right now."
- ○ "I've been burned by other brokers before."
- ○ "I'd like to watch this recommendation first."
- ○ "Send me some information on the stock or your firm."
- ○ "Let me think about it first."
- ○ "Let me speak to my wife about this."

The broker is taught that each of these objections is false; they are merely ways for the prospect to stall for time. The Straight Line says that all these objections must be overcome until the one true objection—the fact that the prospect doesn't know you—can be addressed.

This *objection–rebuttal–power close* sequence is repeated until the prospect relents or hangs up the phone. The call can last 10 minutes or 2 hours. The well-trained broker can use the Straight Line to bring a stray prospect back from any tangent he tries to take the conversation in.

There are prospects who want to buy from the outset but also want to be romanced a bit. There are prospects who truly don't feel comfortable but after 15 minutes of smooth talking are lulled into a sense of familiarity with that voice on the other end of the phone. There are prospects who give everyone a shot regardless of the idea, and then there are those who will never open an account and simply love talking to salespeople. I've seen brokers open accounts with people who were on a cell phone at the airport or standing outside a child's birthday party. Prospects open accounts for a variety of reasons, but the sexiness of being courted by a hotshot broker has almost always been a part of the equation. We were taught that it's the sizzle that sells in a steakhouse, not the meat itself. Now you understand why so many brokers will only pitch men, despite the high percentage of households in which women call the financial shots.

Now that we've covered the philosophy of the pitch, here are the rebuttals and power closes themselves, for the first time ever. I've cleaned up some of the grammar (many brokers are notoriously borderline illiterate), but these are substantially the same texts and scripts that have been secretly handed down from senior to junior broker for decades.

OBJECTION: "LET ME CALL YOU BACK"

The broker trainee is taught that unless the prospect's house is on fire, there's no reason why the call shouldn't proceed.

Call Back 1

"___, I'll give you my 800 number and my fax number. I'll even give you my cell phone and home numbers if you want. But the truth is, you will never call me back.

"It's not because you don't like the idea, but because you have other things to worry about: a business, a life, and more important things than getting back to me, no matter how good my idea is.

"You'll put the idea in the back of your mind and forget about it. Because again, you have other things to worry about.

"___, let me do the worrying for you.

"Give me the same opportunity that you gave your current brokers, a chance to show you what I could do for you."

Call Back 2

"I wouldn't be surprised if, as we're speaking, your secretary is putting a note under your nose. Or you have two people on hold, and another person is waiting outside your office to see you.

"And I also know that the decision to buy this idea or not will not change your life, or for that matter have an impact on the way you live.

"But ___, by having an account here with two of the equity owners and me, I truly feel that this will be the best relationship you will ever have in the market."

Call Back 3

"___, you've already agreed that the idea makes sense, and I'm certain you see that based on these pending announcements, the stock should trade higher.

"However, I think emotionally you can't make the commitment now, am I right?

"___, when do you think most mistakes are made, when people act logically or emotionally?

("Emotionally")

"Exactly!

"Let's not be emotional!

"Let's be logical!"

Call Back 4

"___, I understand you'd prefer to call me back, but let me ask you a question.

"What more are you going to know tomorrow that you don't know already?

"Please ask the questions now. I'll stay on the phone with you until you are satisfied!

"I know that someone as busy as you are will be difficult to get back on the phone with. I don't want to miss this opportunity!

"As you know, ___ currently has a strong buy and is moving its institutional clients into ___ as we speak!"

OBJECTION: "I DON'T LIKE THE MARKET RIGHT NOW"

One of the first lessons the broker-trainee is taught is that the broader market doesn't matter so long as your individual stock selection is good. Of course, once you actually do the research, you learn that, in fact, actually the opposite is true; most of a stock's performance can be attributed to the action in its sector and then the overall market.

Market 1

"___, I understand that you are concerned about the overall market. I wouldn't invest in the broader market right now either.

"However, the state of the market is always relative. I mean, I'm not asking you to buy an index fund on the S&P, am I?

"Of course not!

"I'm asking you to give me a shot on a small trade in an individual, special situation . . . one that looks to trade higher regardless of what happens with the Dow Jones Industrial Average!"

Market 2

"Let me read you a quote from one of the most successful money managers of our time, Sir John Templeton:

You must do something different from the majority. The time of maximum pessimism is the time to sell! Therefore, the only way to find bargains is to buy what most people are selling. Profit is made by focusing on value, not outlooks or trends.

"We have been speaking about optimum value, in both the company we're buying and the relationship we're entering."

Market 3

"___, I understand that right now you don't like the market, but with all due respect, what do you do for a living?

"OK, so you seem to be good at what you do. You know your business, right?

"Well, I know mine!

"I eat, sleep, and breathe this business. I do this 7 days a week and work 12- to 14-hour days. I also happen to work alongside some of the sharpest, most insightful people in the business.

"Establishing an account with me right now gives you the opportunity to benefit from their experience as well as my own.

"Believe me when I say, we know what we're doing in any market conditions."

Market 4

"___, the state of the market is always relative. I wouldn't invest in the broad market averages.

"We're not investing in the market . . . we're investing in an individual, special situation that, relative to the market, should be bought at this level.

"___, big money is made during bad markets, not great markets. I'm not smart enough, nor is anyone on Wall Street smart enough, to pinpoint a bottom. One thing I can tell you, however, is that this is certainly not the top.

"___, when nobody will touch them, then I'll be all over them. When the market is high and sexy, everyone's buying. That's when I'll be selling our stock to them . . . at much higher prices!"

Market 5—McDonald's Rap

"___, the dynamics of the market never change. For a hundred years clients have been telling their brokers yes or no.

"In 1966, McDonald's was a new issue at $22 a share. An investment of just $20,000 would now be worth over $20 million!

"We both know that on that day in 1966, some clients told their brokers they weren't looking to do anything that day, or they never heard of McDonald's, or they just didn't like the market in general.

"The world is made up of two types of people: those who seize opportunity and those who walk through life without a clue.

"No one becomes as successful as you or me without realizing that fact."

OBJECTION: "I'M NOT LIQUID RIGHT NOW"

Broker-trainees are taught to help the prospect "find the money" at all costs, even if that means not only persuading someone to buy a stock but also convincing him to sell something else he owns on the same call.

Not Liquid 1

"___, I understand that you're not feeling as liquid as you'd like to be. I hear that a lot from my clients. But what I find out afterward is what they're really saying is that they are just not as liquid as they might normally be.

"If you were a client of mine for three years and I already had most of your assets under management and was now asking for you to add another quarter of a million, that would be one thing.

"But that's hardly the case here, am I right?

"What I am asking you to do is take ___, probably less than 1 percent of your total assets, and extend to me the same courtesy that you gave to that other broker that's managing the bulk of your money, the one shot.

"Besides, for someone like you, I know that ___ is not a question of yes or no, of whether or not you can do it. It's more a matter of which account to write the check on.

"Am I right?"

Not Liquid 2

"___, I can appreciate the fact that you weren't waiting for a phone call from me with your checkbook open, but liquidity is a very relative statement.

"Let me explain.

"Sometimes if I have a client that usually puts $100,000 into an idea and today he only has $25,000, he doesn't feel liquid. Or one of my big boys that put a million into each and every idea only has $200,000, he also doesn't feel liquid.

"And what I'm getting at is that liquidity right now is completely irrelevant. You and I are going to start real small, on a dollar figure that is insignificant to you—something I know you can handle."

Not Liquid 3

"___, I sense you're being very sincere, and I appreciate that.

"However, I take what I do very seriously. I'm never going to call you when I think you're sitting on the most cash or when I can make the most commission for myself, but only when I have a stock that I believe goes much higher in the short term.

"The amount of this investment is much less important than you seeing our approach.

"The reason for this call is to give you the advantage of our timing.

"___, buying ___ may seem like a big decision, but really, I'm just asking you to take a small step and I will do the rest."

Not Liquid 4

"___, if you're not liquid for 5 or 10 thousand right this second, that's OK. I don't always have 10 grand lying around my office either!

"What's your favorite sport?

"Imagine yourself the manager of your local ___ team. You have just been offered the chance to take on ___, but it means you will have to let go of a mediocre player.

"Would you make the change?

"Of course!

"That's exactly what I'm asking you to do here. Look at the stocks you own right now. I know some of them are down for the count.

"Take a gun and shoot the wounded!

"Redirect the assets into something that you have already agreed makes sense."

OBJECTION: "I'VE BEEN BURNED BY OTHER BROKERS BEFORE"

We were taught that this is the only true objection and the one that all the others actually boil down to—the simple fact that the prospect doesn't know us and that there are so many horror stories out there. These rebuttals are delivered in a manufactured tone of sincerity and often involve the broker climbing under his desk so that the frenetic background noise of the selling floor around him will be muted.

Burned 1

"___, I can certainly appreciate the fact that you've had a bad experience before, and I realize that you may not be familiar with exactly who we are.

"Quite frankly, the reason is that we don't advertise during the Super Bowl. Our reputation has been built on word of mouth and personal service.

"What you need to know right off the bat is that _____ is one of the largest independent money management houses on The Street. We have several offices and branches across the country.

"My place of business is the corporate headquarters in Manhattan, literally surrounded by every major investment bank, hedge fund, and brokerage firm that you've ever heard of.

"___, you are familiar with (well-known clearing firm name) I'm sure, correct? That's my bank clearing agent. Your checks are made payable to them, and your account is insured for up to _____ dollars.

"Before you send a dime anywhere, whether it's our first transaction or our hundredth transaction, you will always receive standard confirmations from a well-known clearing company, which, by the way, manages about *$5 trillion* for investors worldwide."

Burned 2

"___, I can understand that you've been burned before. It happens, unfortunately, and I'll tell you why:

"People get burned because they buy things they don't know about.

"Now if I got on the phone with you and started yelling and screaming about some nonsense penny stock, do you know what you're supposed to tell me?

"You're supposed to tell me to get lost!

"I'm not doing that. I'm asking you to buy one of the most undervalued companies in the market. With ___ in revenue and contracts with companies like ___ and "___, I'm sure you can see the difference, am I right?

"Of course you do!"

Burned 3

"___, here's the problem that I find so often. It's education! Obviously, you're not in the brokerage business. Let me ask you a question. Just out of curiosity, what business are you in? Well, when it comes to that business, I'm sure you probably know all the quality players and all the low-end players. So when you make a decision on whom you want to work with, for the most part you're making an educated decision, am I right?

"Unfortunately though, on Wall Street, you have these very aggressive young men getting into this business without any education or previous business experience. They go to small over-the-counter firms and call you on the phone with whatever stock they are told to push at that time. They bring you some fascinating story that may sound very exciting, maybe they push your greed buttons by telling you that you're going to make 1,000 percent on your money in a month. But the end result is that you are getting pie in the sky.

"But coming from the ___ industry, you don't know if they provide quality or not. So what happens? Because they may sound very good, you end up putting your trust in them and getting killed. My biggest problem in the last ___ years hasn't been making my clients money, it's been trying to keep them from losing money in positions just like that. And that's exactly what I'm trying to prevent you from ever doing again by stopping the buck here.

"Understand something, ___. The dollar amount we work with is of no consequence. You tell me what makes you feel comfortable, and that's what we'll do. But one thing I will assure you of. By the end of the year, after you see the performance of ___, and you see the level of professionalism I provide all my clients, you're going to say, 'Thank God, I've finally found a broker I can rely on!'

"All my clients have said that at one point or another. Then you'll reflect back to this day and realize that you just made the smartest business decision you ever made in the market.

"___, I have one shot and only one shot to make a first impression. And believe me, I've done my homework. Give me the shot this one time and believe in me. I'm not going to let you down."

Burned 4

"I understand why you feel the way that you do. And I know you've heard horror stories about people having bad experiences over the phone with independent firms.

"However, ___, there are major differences between those firms and mine.

"Those firms will open the account with you on a NYSE company that is a well-known name like Home Depot or Toys 'R' Us.

"Then they come to you with a $5 IPO—give you a small piece but make you commit to buying 10 times the amount of stock in the aftermarket—usually you're buying that additional stock between 12 and 15! At the end of the day, the IPO company is raising more money than it's doing in revenues! The stock opens at 15, and six months later it's at 2 bucks a share and the broker stops taking your phone calls.

"My firm specializes in small- and mid-cap stocks, typically profitable companies trading on both the NASDAQ and NYSE. We don't underwrite IPOs, and we only bring investment banking deals that are being spearheaded by the major firms. Our lack of in-house bankers guarantees you the protection against conflicts of interest that have become so prevalent on The Street.

"In addition, nothing we ever come to you with will ever have my firm as a market maker. We hold *zero* inventory in stocks and use every trading skill at our disposal to obtain the best possible prices for clients on the open market."

OBJECTION: "I'D LIKE TO WATCH THIS RECOMMENDATION FIRST"

As more investors began using the Internet, this response became more and more common. The broker-trainee was taught to emphasize the "relationship" as opposed to the eventual performance of the stock, thus negating any of the benefits of watching a recommended trade.

Watch It 1

"I can appreciate the fact that you want to watch the stock, and I'm flattered that you would take the time to track one of my recommendations that you don't even have a vested interest in.

"However, I'm sure you've seen all those mutual fund commercials that say 'past performance doesn't guarantee future results.'

"Am I right?

"___, when I am dead right on this idea, that will not necessarily mean that you'll jump into my next idea blind, am I right?

"Of course you wouldn't.

"You will need to judge each of my recommendations on their own merit, not on the performance of the recommendation that came directly before it!

"And you yourself said that this idea made sense and that you see the opportunity to make money here!"

Watch It 2

"___, can I say one thing?

"Watching this stock go from A to Z is a worthless academic exercise. Nobody has ever made money watching stocks. It only allows me to say I told you so, and that's not my style!

"Mr. ___, we both know that the only thing that will establish a track record for me is a buy confirmation on your desk at ___, and more importantly, a sell confirmation down the road at ___.

"Wouldn't you agree?

"Of course!"

Watch It 3

"___, you're right. You don't have to buy ___ today. Let's say you open the *Journal* three months from now and you see the stock trading higher, substantially higher.

"You're not going to cry because you could have made 5 to 10 thousand on the trade. However, what you will realize is that you lost a broker who knows what the hell he's doing.

"The law of averages says that you have to sift through 100 brokers before you find the one who makes you money on a consistent basis.

"If you knew whom you were talking to, I mean really knew, you'd be buying size right now!

"But I understand that's not the case. I have to do my job, which is basically two main tasks:

- ○ "I have to make you money. With this idea, I think that's the easy part.

- ○ "I have to make you feel comfortable. That's a little more difficult.

"The size of the trade is unimportant to me. Whether you own 100 shares or 10,000 shares, when the stock goes from ___ to ___, you're going to ring the register.

"I'm not asking you to dive in headfirst, just dip your toe in the water and get your feet wet."

Watch It 4

"___, how many calls from brokers do you get per week?

"So that means that you hear about ___ new ideas every week. Do you think that you really have the time to follow stocks that you do not even own in your own portfolio?

(Yes)

"So you follow every stock that is given to you by a broker, and then first keep track of your own holdings? I doubt it!

"It's hard enough to manage your own accounts, you certainly don't have the luxury of worrying about an invisible portfolio of stocks that you don't even own!

"What I am saying is, let me do the worrying for you!

"Besides, for someone like you, 500 or 1,000 shares is almost like watching it! However, it does allow me to get the information on us out to you, and it lets you receive a monthly statement from ___, my bank clearing agent.

"It also allows you to enjoy the ride in a small way!"

Watch It 5

"___, I know that one's initial reaction is to want to watch the first idea, and if it goes higher, try the next one. But I think we're missing the point of what I am really trying to do.

"Let me explain:

"Have you ever bet on a football game or any other sporting event?

("No")

"Have you ever put a friendly wager on anything in your life?

("Yes")

"I bet you watched it a lot closer when you had at least something riding on it, right?

"That's exactly what I'm asking you to do here. Put a little something behind ___!

"Establish an account here with us. Allow us to get you out the monthly statement and showcase our talents, let us show you the professionalism we provide.

"Take a chance on ___!

"I won't let you down."

OBJECTION: "SEND ME SOME INFORMATION ON THE STOCK OR YOUR FIRM"

This objection has morphed from mail me some research to fax it to e-mail it or let me look it up myself on the Internet. In any of those cases, the broker's response zeroes in on how dated anything in print is and how anything that can be mailed out has already been baked into the price of the investment.

Send Info 1

"___, I can appreciate the fact that you want to see something in black and white. Maybe if someone called me today with an idea, I'd react the same way.

"But let me say this to you . . . I have a lot of information on ___. I am looking at a file sitting on my desk that must be about 6 inches thick.

"You see, ____, we've already done our homework on ___.

"The money managers and analysts that I work with have met with the company and its entire management team.

"We have sat in on every conference call and attended every road show and conference appearance that ___ has made over the past few weeks.

"We have a research staff that has ripped apart the company's balance sheet and income statement and examined every fundamental and technical factor there is.

"The real difference here is that we are not a supermarket of stocks. We only make a select amount of recommendations a year, so when I bring you a situation, it will only be something we know firsthand.

"As I mentioned earlier, we are expecting major announcements on the company shortly, and if I thought the best time to buy the stock was two days from now, believe me, I would have waited two days before I called you."

Send Info 2

"___, I understand you want to see some information. Let me ask you a question. What exactly do you want to see?

"An S&P report?

"A chat room on the Internet?

"With all due respect, I know there is a lot of information out there and I know that you're a savvy investor, but there is a lot more to this recommendation than anything that might catch your eye in one of these reports.

"If it were that easy to make money in the market, then I'd be out of the job and everyone would be rich, including the secretaries that type the reports!

"Am I right?

"*Exactly!*

"My firm spends enormous amounts of time and money on these ideas, and I know that our relationship is going to hinge on the success and accuracy of our research on this situation today."

Send Info 3

"I can understand why you want to see information, and I can send you anything that you need. But that's not how you make money in the market.

"You could look at earnings.

"You could look at assets, the balance sheet, all of which are important.

"But they all disclose a company's *past performance.*

"Now in the past when I've taken a company with good earnings and a strong balance sheet, I've made my clients money.

"But when I've timed it with a major near-term event, I've made them a fortune!

"___, you have to agree that a major contract announcement combined with a buy recommendation from a wirehouse firm could only drive the stock higher, right?

"Well, we think you'll see this any day now."

Send Info 4

"I can appreciate the fact that you'd rather see the information first, before making a decision. But I'm sure you agree with me that showing you glowing reports and a buy recommendation from ___ does not guarantee that you will make money on this idea.

"Am I correct?

"*Exactly!*

"The only thing that will make you money here is my timing, and believe me, there is a definite timeliness to this call.

"If just one of the major announcements we're looking for gets out over the tickertape, you and I are paying a lot higher for the stock."

OBJECTION: "LET ME THINK ABOUT IT FIRST"

This was one of the hardest objections to overcome, as everyone's time to think things over is quantitatively different. Broker-trainees became proficient in stressing the urgency of the situation in order to make the act of thinking things over out of the question.

Think about It 1

"___, I can see why you'd want to think it over before making a decision, but also you and I both know that the best time to make a decision is when you have all the facts fresh in your mind, am I right?

"I have just gone over a very thorough presentation in which you yourself agreed that the idea makes sense and the stock should trade much higher. I don't care about the size of our first transaction. I only care about the timing.

"I would rather see you own ___ shares right now at this price than maybe 5 or 10 thousand shares tomorrow or next week at a higher price!

"And if there's even just one question that I can't answer for you on ___, then I don't even want you to own a stitch of stock."

Think about It 2

"___, it seems that your reaction is a very common reaction with my newer accounts and referrals. I mean, let's face it: we've been following ___ for 6 months, and you've only heard of it for maybe 60 seconds.

"But this is the same type of conversation that we had with many newer accounts on an earlier recommendation of a company called ___.

"We gave this recommendation to all the new accounts and referrals here at the firm, and aside from being a great company, in less than ___ weeks, it released blockbuster news to The Street, and we rode the stock from ___ to ___!

"Our clients that made a decision based on our timing made a small fortune, while those that chose to think about it missed out!

"As I mentioned earlier, we are expecting two major announcements any day."

Think about It 3

"___, I can appreciate the fact that you want to think about it. We don't make quick decisions either. But would you agree with me that price and timing are both critical factors when making an investment?

"Of course they are!

"We know our business, and our performance is simply the credential on The Street.

"___, we are bringing you an opportunity, not history, and I am concerned because you must realize that you can't check the kind of advice that we are going to give you.

"By the time you are reading about this on the front page of the *Journal*, we both know it's too late."

Think about It 4

"___, I know that you would feel more comfortable if we had the luxury of thinking about ___ for the next couple of days. And you know what? Maybe ___ even stays at a buying level for another three or four days.

"But what's really important here is showing you a true level of professionalism.

"We only come to you when we have something that we feel is truly exceptional. You don't want to get back to me . . . you want to make real money!

"Under these circumstances, the decision to buy should not be postponed. You should own ___ at the same time as our institutional clients."

Think about It 5—Not Today

"Do you want to know why you're saying not today? Because you can't think of a better reason not to own this company. I sound too good, and the scenario makes too much sense. On top of that, you're not in the mood to buy stock.

"Unfortunately, some of the best opportunities come along when you're not in the mood. I don't call my clients when their bank accounts are the fullest or when I can earn the most commission for myself or for that matter when they're in the mood to buy stock. I come to them when I believe I have a security that trades higher in the near term.

"Six months from now you'll be in a good mood, a buying mood. You may even be more liquid than you are today. Some 22-year-old kid reading from a script, from one of the wirehouses, will sell you with some crazy, sexy, exciting story. You'll be in a buying mood, and you'll buy the stock. You know what? You'll lose your money.

"Give me the one shot, it's the right thing to do."

Think about It 6—First of the Year

"___, you know what? Right now what you're saying is a very common reaction for the small investor.

"Institutions, on the other hand, do not work this way.

"What I mean is you're never going to bring a top fund manager a compelling situation where you both agree that the idea is exceptionally undervalued and have him say to you, 'I'll wait until next year,' or 'call me after tax season.'

"Top fund managers understand the fact that good situations do not always present themselves when it is most convenient.

"That's why it is usually so difficult for the small investor to keep up with the institutions in the market and see comparable results on a consistent basis."

OBJECTION: "LET ME SPEAK TO MY WIFE ABOUT THIS"

The dreaded "let me talk to my wife" objection was where the implied chauvinism of the average broker really got its moment to shine and become a bit more overt. While the rebuttals were worded with some civility, they were delivered in the most mocking and emasculating tone that could be employed without going over the line.

Speak to Wife 1

"I understand why you would want to check with your wife. I have to respect a man who respects his wife. It's probably the reason why I've been with my wife for so long.

"However, as a businessman, which you obviously are, you must make a lot of important decisions everyday, correct?

"Decisions that I'm sure you couldn't or wouldn't consult your wife on! And she's OK with that because she trusts your judgment, right?

"Now if this call was about buying a large piece of property or taking a million-dollar position in a stock, that would be one thing. But we're not talking about anything as substantial as that, are we?

"Of course not!

"What we are talking about, I mean really talking about, is establishing a relationship with someone that you can trust.

"And besides, ___, I know from experience that it's probably a lot easier to beg for forgiveness than it is to ask for permission!"

Speak to Wife 2

"___, I know you'd rather speak to your wife, and believe me, I want you to feel comfortable as well.

"But I know from experience that your wife will feel much more comfortable when you show her the FedEx package that comes to your home after you purchase the stock.

"In it will be a full dossier on ___, as well as a complete profile on me and on the firm. In addition, it will have account information from ___, the largest clearing firm on the planet, which is where your stock is held, not to mention where your checks go to as well. You'll also get the annual report, the 10K, the confirmation, all of which will be much better than you just telling your wife that you want to buy stock from someone you've never spoken to in a company you've never heard of.

"___, what do you think she's going to say?

"*Exactly!*"

Speak to Wife 3

"Let me explain the way I see the conversation going. If you set aside five minutes to speak about it tonight, you'll tell her some guy from New York called you on the phone and wants you to send him 5 or 10 thousand to buy some stock.

"She'll ask you what company.

"You'll tell her ___.

"Either she hits you over the head with a frying pan, or you're sleeping on the couch tonight!

"Either way, she didn't have the chance to make the decision with all the facts. You said you like the idea and see the opportunity to make money.

"What I'm saying is this: You position yourself and your wife in ___ shares now. I know she will respect your decision on a small trade. Then sit down with her, review the FedEx package, and make the decision to work larger together.

"Besides, that whole conversation, I'm sure, happened with a few companies over the past few years like an Intel or a Microsoft, before they became the powerhouses that we know of today."

POWER CLOSES

There were a dozen power closes that the broker-trainee was expected to know backward and forward before getting on the phone with a stock idea. Power closes were used to wrap things up and ask for an order after using a rebuttal to put a prospect's objection to bed. The Third Reich itself would have been impressed with the efficiency of it all.

Power Close 1

"Let me ask you a question.

"If I had been a broker for the past few years making you money on a consistent basis, would it be fair to say you'd be a bit less hesitant?

(*"No"*)

"You mean to tell me that if I had positioned you in ___ and within ___ it was trading at ___, you wouldn't take something here?

"Of course you would!

"Now I understand I don't have the luxury of a track record with you, but that's all I'm looking to establish here today.

"Let me take a step back . . . what you do know is my name: _____. What you don't know is that I work with the top team of partners here at (brokerage firm name). Our team runs the retail and institutional divisions at the firm. It also contains some of the most successful brokers and analysts on Wall Street. We didn't get to this position by being wrong all too often, or by any means working on small trades.

"However, in an effort to make you feel a bit more comfortable since you like the idea, let's do this: start small, we'll pick up a block of ____shares, a cash outlay of ____dollars.

"It's a bit less than we originally spoke about, and you'll make less money as the stock trades higher, but you're percentage gains remain exactly the same. You judge me on that and that alone, and I think the biggest problem we're going to have is that you didn't pick up more!

"Is the ____ shares OK, or would you like to take a stronger position?"

Power Close 2

"I sense you're being a bit more conservative right now because you don't know me, am I correct? I'm a very conservative broker myself. I promise you, I didn't get to this position by not taking into account my clients' downside risk.

"Hypothetically, if we picked up___ shares, and the stock drops ___ points, and you lose ___ dollars, is that going to make you a poor man? Of course not, or I wouldn't be on the phone with you!

"Now, when I'm right and the stock trades to ____ like we think it will, and you make ___dollars, is that going to make you a rich man?

"*Exactly!*

"I'm not getting rich either! My commission, after I split it with the firm and the government—I can't even buy myself lunch!

"This is to serve as a benchmark, to show that I can guide you into the market at the right time—more importantly guide you out at the right time.

"_____, let's do this. Open the account for ____shares, a cash outlay of _____dollars. Give me the shot on a small trade in a great company. If you're not completely satisfied with my level of professionalism and timing over the next 60 to 90 days, I urge you to call me up and fire me as your broker. I'll sell the stock and send you back your proceeds, we'll part as friends.

"On the other hand, when I'm right, and I put a buy confirmation on your desk at ____ and a sell confirmation at _____, I want you to work bigger and better on my next idea.

"*Do just ___ shares. If you like what I do for you on this, we'll work bigger and better down the road, OK?*"

Power Close 3

"Let me ask you a question. If I put you into ___ at ___ and the stock drops like a rock to ___, would you ever listen to me again?

("Yes")

"*You'd listen, but you wouldn't buy!*

"Now on the flipside, say the stock goes from ___ to ___. I think it's fair to say that you'd be a bit less hesitant and you'll want to work bigger and better on my next idea, am I right?

"*Exactly!*

"What I'm saying is this, I have one shot to make you money. That's it. I love baseball, but I'm not a baseball player. I don't get the three strikes. If I blow it, I've blown a relationship for the long term.

"Give me that one shot. Pick up ___shares, a cash outlay of ___ dollars. Judge me for the next 60 to 90 days on my pricing and timing, and the only regret you're going to have is that you didn't know me well enough to buy the original ___ shares.

"Stretch with me this one time on ___, and I'll never have to ask you to stretch again!"

Power Close 4

"___ , the reason I've been so successful with my clients is because I like to put things on a scale.

"Your downside on ___ shares is roughly ___ dollars. Your upside is not the few grand that you stand to make here on ___. Your upside is establishing a relationship with a top Wall Street broker who's made a fortune for his clients time and time again.

"Obviously, it hasn't happened on a couple hundred or even a couple thousand shares of any stock, but on three or four carefully selected investment banking opportunities:

1. When my clients are liquid

2. More importantly, when my performance warrants it

"Do this: pick up ___ shares, and give me the next 60 to 90 days. If you're not satisfied with the performance of the stock, or with me for that matter, like I said, you call me up and tell me to sell the stock and send you a check, end of story.

"But when the stock performs as I say it will, you promise me that we will never work at these small levels again . . .

"Work with me on ___ shares. You won't be disappointed!"

~

So there you have it. The methodology of the Straight Line, the rebuttals to every specific objection, and some of the power closes that have been designed to get you from no to yes. One of the fundamental reasons why brokers in general can't make you money is that they spend a majority of their day practicing, delivering, or training others in this very pitch.

And if some of the lines sound corny or hokey, keep in mind that *corny* works. *Hokey* sells stocks and opens up accounts.

PART FOUR

THE PROMISE

"Everyone has a plan, 'til they get punched in the mouth."
—Mike Tyson

*"Well, you know, I was a human being before
I became a businessman."*
—George Soros

"I come back to you now at the turn of the tide."
—Gandalf, *The Lord of the Rings*

21

Staying Out of the Murder Holes

There are some stock market land mines that will invariably destroy anyone foolish enough to stand on them for an extended period of time.

My friend The Fly, an anonymous blogger who writes the popular if misanthropic trading Web site iBankCoin, has a term he likes to use for these. He calls them *murder holes,* and a more apt description for these investments couldn't be conjured if Shakespeare himself came out of a creative writing workshop and checked his portfolio. I think the term was (relatively) recently popularized when it was used in *Saving Private Ryan,* but it perfectly describes the types of investments we're about to discuss.

Until you've been blown up by a few of these murder holes yourself, it's hard to recognize them. Below is a list of the dark alleys you never want to wander down for your own future financial well-being.

These alleys are strewn with various land mines, any of which could become your very own murder hole at any time. You probably won't listen anyway, but don't say I didn't warn you.

SPACs. NASA engineers working at full tilt for 18 months couldn't draw up a worse product than what a handful of investment banks began selling to retail customers in the mid-2000s. SPAC stands for *special-purpose acquisition corporation,* but it may as well mean *selling promises and craziness.* The basic premise of the SPAC is this:

- ○ We put together a board of directors that has a great business pedigree (the former CEO of this, the ex-chairman of that, etc.).
- ○ We go public and raise a big pile of cash that we have a year or so to put to use.
- ○ The bankers bring us acquisition candidates until we pick one.
- ○ We buy the company and change our name from the SPAC to the company's name, and our directors and execs assume those roles at the newly merged entity.
- ○ Now you are a shareholder in an operating business that we have bought. Congrats!

Sounds interesting, right? The reality is that it sucks for everyone except the investment bankers. Here's the deal . . .

For starters, promising companies with no flies on them are able to just go public the regular way through a traditional IPO. They don't need to be backdoored into the market via a merger with a SPAC. Only the dregs of the private company barrel need to do a deal like this to hit the public markets. American Apparel (APP) is one example; it is one of the most disastrous stocks of the past decade. The founder and CEO was not only accused of cooking the books; he also had a history of sexually tormenting the barely legal models who worked for him.

Another thing to keep in mind is that many well-known and respected corporate chieftains have merely been lucky; they are not automatically going to succeed at ventures. Look at Microsoft's Paul Allen as an example. Here's a guy who, once he left the software company that made him one of the world's wealthiest men, couldn't wait to set fire to his cash. Everything he touched turned to compost. It was almost as though he was in some kind of *Brewster's Millions* type of situation where he had to blow $5 billion in order to inherit $50 billion. There are lottery winners from log cabins in the back woods who've been smarter with their investments.

So anyway, a SPAC trots out someone like Steve Wozniak (from Apple), and it makes a deal to buy some also-ran company like Jazz Semiconductor. Yay! Wrong, you will lose. The same thing went on with the hapless losers who ran Jamba Juice into the ground and countless other SPAC stories over the years. No one who invests in these things makes any money—before the merger or after it.

Also, hedge funds typically are hooked up with shares from the SPAC's IPO. They will bail the moment there is any kind of premium in the stock price over that initial cash-per-share amount the company raised. You will be holding the bag, señor, not them.

According to Reuters, the last big wave of 57 SPACs that debuted at the height of the credit bubble in 2007 had raised a combined $11.3 billion. That's a whole lot of "dumb money." The best thing that could've transpired for those 57 companies would have been the return of cash that occurs when the clock runs out and a deal hasn't been consummated. In fact, there were a few hedge funds involved with some of those SPACs that were forcing that dissolution to occur using the voting power of their stock positions.

Finally, let's understand what this vehicle really is—a way for investment bankers to pay themselves multiple times. First, they take the SPAC public; that's a fee. Then they consult for the company on retainer as a potential acquisition is sought, another banking fee.

OK, they've found a company for the SPAC to buy. Guess what? Another fee, a big one this time. Then there is the arduous 12-month process during which the SPAC seeks shareholder and regulatory approval for the deal. Fees, fees, fees. Finally, the deal is closed. Now of course, the SPAC has probably bitten off more than it could chew, and so a secondary stock offering or some kind of convoluted debt or warrant offering needs be done. You guessed it, another round of fees. The SPAC structure is an ATM machine for the bankers. And how have the investors done? Murdered. Like *down 80 percent* murdered. If it weren't so true, it would almost be laughable how horribly and slowly these things die. And by the way, many of these SPACs have been China-related in recent years. For investors, the China-SPAC combination is like being beaten up after school and then coming home to find that your parents have moved away without telling you.

And just so you know, the investment banks that make these stepchild IPOs are almost always connected to an aggressive brokerage sales force. How else could $100 million be raised for such a harebrained scheme?

Chinese Reverse Mergers. Nobody does accounting fraud like China. It should come as no surprise that small corporations from a country that invents its own GDP statistics are themselves cooking the books. What's adorable is that much of the fraud in U.S.-listed Chinese small caps is aspirational in nature; three company-owned shipping facilities become six in the quarterly filing, $50 million in revenues becomes $60 million . . . who's going to know the difference? Corporate China's worst element meets the underworld of the U.S. banking complex, and together they release hundreds of scams onto the American Stock Exchange, the NASDAQ, and even the once prestigious NYSE.

Here's how it works: Let's say that you are a Chinese business owner looking to raise investment capital. You happen to read and hear about how foolishly U.S. investors are being herded into all manner of "emerging market" investments. Well, you want your piece too, don't you? So you make contact with a U.S.-based investment banker (these bankers are crawling all over China these days), and a deal is struck to "take you public" on a U.S. exchange. The first thing that happens is that a shell company with a public stock but no actual business operations is located on either the Pink Sheets or the Bulletin Board market. Why these things are even permitted to trade is beyond me, but fine, there are tons of shells for sale. You then work with a law firm or accounting outfit that specializes in the reverse merger of your company into the shell. Your corporate filings are upgraded so that they pass muster with the exchanges, and you are leapfrogged from one to the next until you can get to the big show— the NASDAQ. At this point, you will have added tens of millions in market cap as more investors hear your story—"They are the leading provider of dried seafood snacks in all of Guangdong Province!" And while your business may be legitimate, there's a good chance that your accounting is a circus wrapped in a carnival.

And then a short seller tugs a few loose threads, and before you know it, your stock craters. It is eventually delisted, and everyone is crushed.

Bloomberg keeps an index of these Chinese RTO stocks (RTO meaning *reverse takeover*). This index was essentially cut in half during the first half of 2011, as fraudulent companies large and small were dismantled by intrepid short sellers and fleeing investors (see Figure 21.1). Even John Paulson, one of the most successful investors in history, had gotten himself caught in a Chinese fraud called Sino-Forest. Media reports had estimated that Paulson's losses on the way out of the pump-and-dump timber stock may have been in the $700

Figure 21.1. *Interactive Chart*

million range. Even in the context of a $37 billion hedge fund, losses of that magnitude will leave a mark.

The short sellers who have attacked and unmasked the Chinese RTO fraud machine have done investors a favor in the long run. I've advised people to avoid the entire China stock sector until the companies grow up a bit and start acting like professionals. After all, if the legendary John Paulson can be taken in by these charlatans, what chance do you have?

One-Drug Biotechs. One of the great things about the U.S. capital markets is that a small biotechnology company with nothing other than some scientists and a promising protein compound can be a publicly traded company while it tests and proves the efficacy of a drug. But while this is a testament to the strength and depth of our capital markets, it doesn't mean that you'd want your own capital to be in harm's way like that. One of the easiest mistakes to avoid in the stock market is believing in a biotech story too early and for too long. After all, the vast majority of drug trials fail to satisfy the FDA, and approvals are the exception, not the rule.

According to a *Wall Street Journal* report, the FDA approved just 26 new drugs in 2009 of which only 7 were biotechnology compounds. The year before, there were 25 new drug approvals with only 4 of them from the biotech arena. How do those odds sound to you as a betting person? How about as an investor in one of the 400 or so small and midsized biotechs with under a billion dollars in market cap? One of the evergreen pieces of investing advice that almost all of the masters agree with is to stack the odds in your favor when entering an investment. With one-drug biotechs, you are willfully doing the opposite.

Retail brokers love to pitch these things because the stories sound incredible and the potential percentage gains are in the four-digit range when they work. Unfortunately most of them don't, like 19 out of 20. And when they fail, it's not like shareholders have the chance to sell and walk away. The stocks are typically halted preceding the inevitable gap down before the market's open, as investors realize that it's back to the drawing board for the next four quarters. By the time you can sell the stock, it is already reduced to rubble at your feet.

I've seen many a broker blow up an entire book of clients with just a single biotech stock that failed to get approval. The broker typically will spend a weekend in Atlantic City recovering from a disaster like losing a few million in assets under management, and by Monday morning he is back on the phones. "I'm in rebuilding mode," he tells his desk mates as he smiles and dials with the next sexy story. His clients will probably be called a week later when the broker needs to book a loss and move into something else for the commission. That C Class Benz and the bar tab from Atlantic City certainly aren't going to pay for themselves!

If you must own biotechnology, try to go with a larger company that has several drugs on the market or in development. It may not produce a 10× return, but it also won't vaporize your portfolio on an FDA setback.

Private Placements. Almost every private placement you have ever been pitched or will ever be pitched is a scam. Yes, you heard me correctly. I've witnessed over 200 private placements be brought into brokerage firms, sold to "accredited investors," and then basically disappear into a black hole of unreturned phone calls and shareholder communications that simply stopped coming.

According to *Registered Rep* magazine, just two private placements (Medical Capital and Provident) have been responsible for the shuttering of 21 well-known broker-dealers since 2010. GunnAllen, QA3, Empire Securities, Jesup & Lamont, and Securities America were just some of the casualties when these two diseased privates blew up and took the brokerages' clients with them. Class-action settlements in the tens of millions forced these firms under and left many of the employees without jobs. And these were supposed to have been two of the more reputable deals.

I am fortunate in that I have never in my entire career pitched or sold a private placement. It was pure luck that I had learned very early on to avoid these murder holes, no matter what. In the late 1990s, as an intern at a brokerage firm, I watched as two men made the rounds all over Long Island and Manhattan pitching private shares of Ranch 1, the popular southwestern fast-food chain. They wined and dined brokers from firm to firm during due diligence lunches and boardroom presentations. All the brokers bought in with their clients' money—"It's the next McDonald's," went the pitch, "and you're getting in on the ground floor before it goes public!"

A week later, we found out that the two Ranch 1 representatives were, in fact, just franchisees of a few stores. They had nothing to do with Ranch 1 the corporation. Their documents and private placement memorandum (PPM) packets were a work of fiction. Supposedly, they took all the money they had raised and ran away to Israel. At least that's how the story goes. I never even considered pitching a private placement once I had witnessed that particular debacle; it was all the education I needed.

While this anecdote is an extreme example, the vast majority of private placements end the same way, with a disappearance. The brokers have all been paid their commissions, and the companies that have raised the money aren't expecting any more, and so no one has a vested interest to find out what happened.

So I'll tell you what happens and what will always happen when retail brokers bring their clients private banking deals. By the time a company is desperate enough to go to broker-dealers for funds, it means that it is already at the end of its rope. It can't secure more funding from a commercial bank or a middle-market lender. Its founders and current shareholders are also tapped out. The company has also been rejected by the larger investment banks that have serious corporate finance departments. So the executives put together a PPM, put on clean suits, and do a road show of brokerage firms with a banker or investor relations clown in tow. The retail brokers are offered a 10 percent commission to show the deal to their clients. They are also promised warrants and stock options should the company end up going public (it won't). This exorbitant compensation for the brokers is a huge red flag. "Brown's law of brokerage product compensation" states the following:

> *The higher the commission or selling concession a broker is paid to sell a product, the worse that product will be for his or her clients.*

Using this law as a guideline, a 10 percent commission is off the charts, the brokerage equivalent of someone yanking the emergency cord on a speeding bullet train. Brokers take note: selling a client a private placement that pays you a tenth of that money back is the same thing as telling your client to go f*ck himself.

And by the way, the more interesting the company, the more dangerous the private placement offering. In 2007 Lou Pearlman was sitting in my firm's conference room pitching us his newest venture, Talent Rock, a summer camp for *American Idol* wannabes. If the name Lou Pearlman sounds familiar, it's because he was the producer who first assembled the Backstreet Boys and N*Sync using kids from the Disneyfied song-and-dance ghettos of Orlando, Florida. He had supposedly made around a hundred million dollars or so, and here he was asking for us to call our clients to send him more. In addition to sweating like a pedophile on one of those hidden camera sting shows, he was also completely ludicrous when going over the specifics of his offering. One of my fellow brokers asked him, "If it's true that you're worth a hundred million and own your own private jet, why are you here looking to raise 50 grand?" Pearlman's answer was that he needed to buy out his old partners from the deal and they refused to take money from him. This was so nonsensical that even the troglodytes in the firm who would sell anything to anyone knew it was fishy. Six months later Lou Pearlman was arrested in Germany and extradited back to the United States for this very scam. He had run this Ponzi scheme for years and had raised tens of millions, much of it from retail brokers and their clients.

Another celebrity had come to pitch us a private placement that was supposedly "a sure thing" and on the verge of going public. You had to be in the room to believe this one. Standing in front of a PowerPoint projection screen, and wearing a black blazer with a red rose in the lapel, was the legendary Gene Simmons of the band Kiss. The rocker was sans stage makeup and flanked by a cadre of television and Internet executives as he pitched us on a venture of his called No-Good TV. The premise was that he was starting an Internet and cable TV network that would air all the outtakes of interviews and television shows that contained the naughty bits that regular TV wouldn't broadcast. We were shown clips of Ben Affleck cursing up a blue streak and Colin Farrell's just-leaked sex tape and told that this was "the next HBO." The brokers took pictures with Gene, and one of the sales assistants tried to find out what hotel he was staying at in Midtown. We were given the due diligence packages after the road show, and we laughed like bastards at how ridiculous it all was. Gene went on to launch a TV show on the A&E network that attempted to turn his family into *The Osbournes*. It didn't work, and neither did No-Good TV, thank heavens for the American viewing public.

These days there are huge questions surrounding the selling of private real estate investment trusts (REITs), in which many brokerage firms are currently engaged. The private REIT pays the brokers somewhere around a 7 percent commission on average. And while the real estate holdings and management capabilities of these private REITs may be fantastic, I still couldn't understand why the clients wouldn't be better off investing in one of the hundreds of public REITs. And then a broker explained that because the private REIT is nontraded, it means that "there will be less volatility in the client's portfolio." I know, completely insane. And of course that 7 percent commission is built into the offering price; the client never sees it or feels it (and in many cases doesn't even know about it).

I won't go so far as to say that all private REITs are murder holes, like all private placements are, but I will say to think twice about the advantages of buying a private one when there are scores of perfectly attractive public ones that offer daily liquidity and price discovery.

~

And there are other investor traps out there, too numerous to expound on each of them here. They include:

- Oil and gas limited partnerships. (If you're being cut in on them, the wells are dry.)
- Principal protection funds. (They always come out after the market's been killed and cap your upside on the recovery.)
- Insurance brokers selling asset management. (Does your hairdresser also repair the roof on your house?)
- Stockbrokers selling guaranteed-return equity-linked annuities. (Yeah, that'll end well.)
- Reverse convertibles and other structured products. (They will pit you against both the market *and* the banker—good luck!)
- Brokers with one day left in their pay period. (They will call you with the news that "we need to rotate and move some things around.")
- Brokers with thick New York accents and Boca Raton area codes. (Florida's Homestead Act has led to a preponderance of bad guys from New York setting up shop in southern Florida; the civil courts can't touch their property.)
- Anyone who claims to have a "system." (Why? Because there is no such thing, and if there were, you would be the last person to hear of it.)

- ○ Anyone who calls himself a "financier." (He's guaranteed to be full of sh*t and probably wears a suit and dress shoes with no socks.)

- ○ Financial advisors who self-clear or self-custody client funds. (Always be sure there is another pair of eyes on your money, preferably a large corporation's.)

- ○ Currency brokers and forex sites. (Nobody knows anything; this is all highly leveraged speculation, and the brokers are actually trading against you when you take a position.)

- ○ Managed futures funds. (The fees are so over the top that your actual return will look nothing like the advertised return.)

- ○ Movie investments. (The latest telemarketing scam; no studio worth investing in is going to unleash an army of cold callers to raise funds.)

- ○ Closed-end fund IPOs. (These funds should only be bought at a discount in the secondary market. Within 90 days of the IPO, the "penalty bid" phase ends and brokers can freely dump shares while keeping their commissions—you will be down 15 percent in a blink.)

So much product is being churned out that a financial advisor like myself can feel more like a bouncer than anything else. Lucky for me, I look good in a black t-shirt with my arms folded across my chest. Many of my clients know to run these ideas past me before acting on an aggressive pitch. My answer is almost always no.

I'd love to be wrong, but that hasn't happened yet when dissuading the people I care about from these types of murder holes. Consider yourselves warned.

22

Today and Tomorrow

If way to the Better there be, it exacts a full look at the Worst.
—Thomas Hardy

One of the things I wanted to avoid with this book was to merely write a glamorous advertisement for myself or my practice (mission accomplished). If you were expecting yet another "here's the right way to invest" tome, then I probably disappointed you. But something tells me you've read enough of those.

Wall Street's marketing kung fu is strong, but the truth is stronger. I'm of the belief that as more people understand the way the investment business really works, they can make better choices and become better investors. This is not a book that sets out to create market-beating superstar traders out of Mom and Pop; there are enough people selling that particular dream to the public. This is a book about understanding the disconnects between Wall Street and Main Street.

If I've accomplished this, you now have a good grasp on what I think America needs to know about its investing industry. You should also have a good sense of where I think it's all headed in the future. But my own opinions are only the sum total of the prejudices and experiences that helped to forge them. I wanted to bring in some additional voices to present you with a more panoramic view.

The one thing that everyone seems to agree with is that there is a fundamental problem with the way America and its financial services sector interact with each other. Neither side is entirely innocent. Investors bring fear, greed, unrealistic expectations, intellectual laziness, and impatience to the table. Investment pros too often counter these faults with those of their own, such as conflicted business models, aggressive sales practices, deceitful marketing, and hidden fees. The gap between these two opposing factions of counterproductivity has perhaps never been wider.

I've asked a few friends of mine to help me spell out exactly why it is that this gap continues to grow. They are, in my estimation, the most knowledgeable industry commentators writing today.

Charles Rotblut is a vice president at the AAII and edits the *AAII Journal.* There is no organization that has worked harder to educate and communicate with the investing public over the years. Charles sees the difference between suitability and pragmatism as a core issue facing the industry and its customers. "The biggest disconnect between investors and the investment business is the difference between 'suitability' and 'what is right.' It is in the best interest of investment companies to pitch products that are suitable for a certain investor and profitable. It is in the best interest of the investor to ask 'why is this being pitched,' and question whether it is really a better investment idea than what is already in his portfolio."

Charles doesn't fault the industry for pursuing its goals of higher assets under management and, by extension, more fees. Like me, he accepts that this is the raison d'être of the investment business, and to chide it for being itself misses the more important lesson. His admonition is instead a practical one: "Investment companies exist for one reason, to make money. Investors are under no requirement to help them achieve that goal."

One of the most fundamental problems with the equation as it currently stands is that for many, finance isn't just a foreign language; it may as well exist on a different plane of existence. David Merkel, author of the popular *Aleph Blog*, has worn several hats in the investment business, from investment analyst to life insurance actuary to chief economist and director of research. His take is that "the average person is a saver and not an investor, and has no true knowledge of investing. To them it is magic. Returns occur for unexplainable reasons."

Mark Bruno, the director of online content and data for *Investment News* agrees that a lack of education is behind much of the disconnect. "Without a basic understanding of money, investing and finance, most individuals will struggle to accept or trust the products and services offered by an investment professional. Can it be fixed? Maybe, if we become a more financially literate society. But as it stands, most investors don't know enough about money and investing to either demand or trust the right investment services."

It's important to understand that this lack of education among individual investors can manifest itself in a host of reckless behaviors, some of which are even encouraged by the creators of products in the marketplace. Carl Richards, like me, is both a financial advisor and a blogger. When we talked about this type of recklessness on the part of the inexperienced, he explained that long-term investment success "is far more about behavior than it is about skill." Carl's Web site, Behavior Gap, is known for his Sharpie sketches that both bring market participants back to earth and make us chuckle. An astute follower of the way investors tend to self-sabotage, he believes that "the constant, never-ending search for the next great investment leads us to behavior that actually costs us money!"

There are times when this kind of erratic behavior becomes a marketwide phenomenon as millions of investors are swept up in pursuing a strategy or asset class all at once. Tom Brakke, who writes at the *Research Puzzle* blog, points out that a key reason for this is our natural desire to be where there is money being made right now. He believes that marketing departments encourage this as they "usually promote a product well past the time that it makes sense for their clients, as long as it's an easy sell." Tom is a consultant to investment firms, helping them both design their research processes and communicate their ideas to clients. He explains that this type of continued promotion "proves to be a double whammy for investors, who already are susceptible to the behavioral tendency to chase success. Money pours into the hottest areas and flees from the coldest ones, reinforcing the trends past the point of reasonableness." This chasing of hot trends inevitably leads to "the well-documented result that realized client returns lag the results for the funds themselves (and, of course, those from the cheaper and easier route of passive investing)."

The irony here is that as often as we see the uneducated masses engaging in foolish behavior, it seems that it is the so-called sophisticated investors who tend to find themselves in the deepest trouble at the end of a cycle. Jason Zweig, a legendary financial journalist who has been covering Wall Street for decades, thinks that the term *sophisticated* is a misnomer in and of itself when describing investors. "To invoke George Carlin, the words 'sophisticated investor' have about as much business being stuck together as 'jumbo shrimp,' 'military intelligence' or 'United Nations.' Sophisticated investors start out with more money, but only wise investors end up keeping it. Wisdom has nothing to do with how much money you have, how many graduate degrees you have trailing after your name, or how many algorithms you send marching across your portfolio."

Zweig currently writes the "Intelligent Investor" column for the *Wall Street Journal* and has seen people fall prey to every type of trick, shortcut, and fool's gold rush in the book. While he notes that sophistication alone cannot protect people from The Street or themselves, there are three virtues in particular that can make a difference. "As Benjamin Graham pointed out, intelligence is a function not of your brain but of your character. Independence, skepticism and emotional self-control are the keys to investing success. Being 'sophisticated' has nothing to do with it. The odds that most investors will realize this any time soon—or ever—are statistically indistinguishable from zero."

But character flaws aren't the only reason that so many investors fall short of their goals. As I've pointed out throughout this book, The Street's perpetuation of half-truths and outright myths about investment products and services has been near fatal to the average portfolio. My friend Bill Singer is one of the most well-known legal experts in the securities industry. He says that "the mythology of Wall Street is that the securities industry is primarily concerned about its customers' best interest. This fantasy is cynically promoted to the public by glossy advertising and dubious marketing. The business of Wall Street is about the best interests of the brokerage firm."

Bill frequently comments on brokerage regulatory issues at his blog *Broke and Broker* and as an Intelligent Investing panelist for *Forbes* magazine. Between his time spent at the SEC and his long career representing both brokerage firms and clients, he's had a unique vantage point to see how the industry has changed over the years. "Of decreasing importance with each decade is providing individual, retail clients with superior customer service, competitive commissions, vetted private/public offerings, independent research, and bespoke investment counseling."

While investors are beginning to realize that the investment business is rife with conflict, they are nowhere near an understanding of exactly where that conflict may lie. This may have something to do with the fact there are so many people with so many disparate designations hanging out their shingles these days. As the managing editor of *Registered Rep* magazine, Kristen French can certainly attest to this phenomenon. She tells me that "it's a zoo out there—stockbroker, investment advisor, financial planner, wealth manager, life planner, retirement specialist, these are just a few of the terms investment professionals use to describe themselves. There are so many different breeds of investing professional today and what an investing professional does for the client has changed so much in the past decade, that few investors are clear about who does what in the new landscape or what legal responsibilities these professionals have to their clients."

One of the provisions in the new Dodd-Frank financial reform legislation was for Congress to study the issue of a single fiduciary standard for all investment professionals who deal with the public. This would expand the responsibilities of brokers from the less stringent "suitability" requirement they currently operate under. As of this writing, this unified standard doesn't appear to be imminent or even likely. Kristen says that although legislation may not do the trick, awareness may hold the key. "At this point it's not clear how or when the relevant reforms will actually be implemented. In the meantime, the mainstream media seems to be doing a somewhat better job at explaining how, say, the suitability standard and the fiduciary standard differ in practice."

But there are those of us who have spent enough time inside the belly of the beast to know that there is still the overarching issue of a business model that is broken beyond all repair. Scott Bell had his own break with the traditional broker model years ago, and like me, he's never looked back. He tells me that "investors think their Wall Street advisors are acting as a fiduciary, and in most cases, they're not. This is the single biggest disconnect I see, institutional banking interests doling out individual advice." To Scott, who runs GDP Wealth Management and the blog *I heart Wall Street*, the disconnect is downright systemic, especially at the bulge bracket firms. "Until Wall Street is broken up into smaller specialized pieces: Brokerage, Investment Banking, and Individual Advice, I don't see the incumbents truly changing much. Nor do I see individuals getting the advice advocate they deserve."

There are several outcomes for the future of Wall Street that I see as inexorable. As we've discussed, the ETF will ultimately meet and then exceed the assets under management of the mutual fund complex. The crossing of this particular Rubicon will occur once the nation's largest 401(k) providers begin to really open the gates. Traditional mutual fund families are not waiting around for this inevitability; they are currently building and launching ETF versions of their most popular offerings from their open-end lineup. I've also been pretty unambiguous about the fact that by the time Hollywood makes the movie version of this book, the term *stockbroker* will cease to exist as a profession.

Let's have a look at what my colleagues think is in store for the investment industry . . .

Tom Brakke agrees with me about the effects of the ongoing ETF revolution. "The ETF juggernaut will continue to pressure the mutual fund and separate account businesses, causing significant changes at many investment firms. Paying higher fees for index-hugging managers will make no sense, especially since most fail to outperform over time. The best firms will see the writing on the wall, which should result in increased innovation in investment methods coming to an industry that has been lacking in creativity, other than the alchemy of financial engineering."

David Merkel, who has spent a fair amount of time in the insurance industry, tells us that "distribution products will become mainstream. There will be many scandals over disappointments generated through returns falling short of illustrated levels that were not and could not be guaranteed. This may lead to limits on what financial planners and other entities are allowed to illustrate as returns in financial plans for non-guaranteed elements. Additionally, it is more likely than not that some insurance company will fail after promising high-ish returns on immediate annuities, together with an offshore reinsurer that enabled them to do it."

Scott Bell sees technological advancement as having an even greater impact than it has already. "The disruption from technology has yet to be fully felt by the industry. In the next ten years, I think we'll see continued pressure on margins and lower fees within the industry as technology automates more and more of the services once valued by clients (and done by their advisor)."

Bill Singer thinks that this technological advancement will speed the denouement of Wall Street's physical presence. "The Era of Wall Street as a geographical designation that centered the financial world in Lower Manhattan will fade and we will see more market centers spread out in Asia, Latin America, and elsewhere. Finally, with the increasing internationalization of the securities industry, customers will likely demand quicker and cheaper access to foreign exchanges, which will spur the growth of more unified markets that will eliminate many of the current barriers to international investing by retail clients. The importance of a 'national' identity to a stock exchange will lessen as investors will simply look to sit at their computer, enter trades to buy/sell stocks in China, Brazil, Germany, and the United States on one platform, at one commission rate, and with a uniform settlement and clearing process."

Mark Bruno sees a tremendous opportunity on the horizon for investment managers and individuals alike, one that he says could benefit us as long we aren't too greedy. "Defined benefit pensions are sun-setting. Defined contribution plans are putting money directly in the hands of investors, replacing a promise that was managed at an institutional level. Social Security could go the same route. The net net: Trillions of dollars will be transitioned into accounts controlled by individuals. Individual investors will have more choice, more pricing power and more flexibility as they independently amass wealth. Investment companies and advisors will compete for their assets and individuals should be in a position to have more control and power over their providers."

Kristen French also sees more choice for investors, and along with it, a Pandora's Box of more complexity. "Financial innovation is not going to stop and that well-oiled machine is already up and running and spitting out new asset classes and products—as well it should be. Over the next decade financial products will become more complex and opaque but they will also become more accessible to the retail market. Knowing how to allocate to them to achieve financial goals will require greater sophistication on the part of both financial advisors and clients."

But will regulation keep up with the inevitable parade of new products? Not if we keep regulating in legalese, says Jason Zweig. "I hope the biggest change is that financial regulation stops being written by lawyers for lawyers and we finally get the psychologists involved. Brokers and financial advisers are required by regulations to determine their clients' risk tolerance, even though none of them have the slightest idea how to do it. The issuers of securities are required to disclose risks in their prospectuses, despite scientific evidence that the detailed disclosure of risks makes people more willing to take risks. Flagrant conflicts of interest go unchecked because of the preposterous belief by regulators that disclosing a conflict somehow 'cures' it. The fundamental philosophy of securities regulation—that disclosure gives investors everything they need to make an informed decision—is intellectually bankrupt. It needs to be replaced—the sooner the better—with a philosophy that takes into account the way actual human beings make actual decisions."

I'll leave this discussion of the future with a sentiment from Carl Richards that I think all my colleagues can get behind. "My hope is that somehow the traditional financial services industry will figure out that behind the money there are real people, living in the real world, with hopes and dreams and that helping them make smarter decisions about money is truly a sacred trust."

Amen, Carl.

23

Breakaway

"What do you mean you're leaving?"

"I just . . . I don't know. I can't do this anymore. I can't go into that place anymore."

"Josh, this is scary. We have a house and Tara's school. And Justin's turning one this summer. What are you doing? What are *we* doing?"

"I know what I need to do. I'm leaving. I've spent 10 years doing this sh*t. I can't do it anymore. I can't even think about doing it anymore. It's all bad."

"I understand, but how are we going to live? Do you even have a plan?"

"I don't have a plan yet, but I'm working on it. And I promise that everything's going to be different from now on."

"You always say that."

"I swear to you. I know how to do this the right way. I know what I need to do, I'm *telling* you."

"What about your business?"

"I *have no business!* Just people I sell things to. I can't do it, it doesn't work, it's killing me. Making me sick."

"But Josh, what about your clients?"

"They're coming with me. I won't leave them there."

"*You* won't leave *them*? What if they don't come? Then what?"

"They'll come. They have to come. I need them to come, and they'll come with me."

"I don't know . . ."

"I'm sorry for everything."

"Josh . . ."

"I'm sorry for everything. But everything's going to be OK from now on. I promise things will get better. I'll do whatever it takes. I just need you to believe in me. Please."

"I've always believed in you. OK . . . get out of there and do it. Just do it."

～

It's December 2009. The world had ended nine months earlier, but then it hadn't. People were picking up the pieces a few months later, but my god how close we had come. The S&P 500 hit 666 on the nose one Friday afternoon, and I posted a video of R.E.M. performing "It's the End of the World as We Know It" on my blog. The most conservative accounts I was overseeing—bonds, gold, and blue chips—were down 30 percent. My aggressive accounts, forget about it.

People ask why the clients weren't just put into cash, given how bad things were. *Because I'm a f*cking stockbroker. What am I supposed to do? Put my clients in cash for two years and take my kids to a f*cking soup kitchen? Or should I be shorting the market with people's rollover IRAs?*

I told my father-in-law on the way home from the train station one day that if one more person yelled at me or criticized me in any way that I was going to get up from my desk and just quietly disappear. I'm sure he was thrilled to hear that. I might have been just talking, or I might have been serious; I'm not sure now.

And what I hated more than anything was watching the guys I worked with struggle. I was a co–branch manager during the worst market crash in 70 years. Hardly anyone who was alive had ever experienced anything like it, and here I was at 31 years old trying to help people through it. My bullsh*t brave-face routine and all those stupid, fake pep talks. There were days when I'd come home, but then I'd sit in my car in the driveway instead of actually coming home.

And it must have shown on my face; my friends who were pharmaceutical sales reps or lawyers or whatever didn't want to be around me and couldn't understand how those hyperbolic headlines in the newspaper were actually affecting me in real life. It also could be heard in my voice; you know you sound despondent when clients on the phone are telling you to keep your chin up.

The economy was falling apart, and so was the firm I worked for, and I still had to figure out how to smile around the babies each night and cobble together a paycheck each month.

And then a ray of light named Howard Lindzon burst through the clouds. Lindzon is the venture capitalist founder of StockTwits, the blog network I'm hosted on. "Joshie, we love the blog, and I want you to come out to this thing I do in San Diego called *Lindzonpalooza.* It's a great group of people coming out this year. There are tech guys, Wall Street guys, you gotta come."

In May 2010 I fly out to the Del Coronado Hotel, and I meet one of my idols in the business, Howard's friend Barry Ritholtz. He tells me about how his firm is really ramping up its RIA business. I mention to him that I'm already shopping around at RIAs and looking to get out of the brokerage game once and for all. Barry had foreseen the housing crash and had very loudly predicted its effect on the global economy and stock market. Was it a lucky, one-off call that was made in passing? Well, he only wrote about 6,000 blog posts on the subject in the year leading up to it, so *you tell me.* Anyway, when I get back to New York City, there's an e-mail from Barry, and within a week I am plotting my escape from hell.

The move wasn't easy, as I've discussed earlier, but then I'd never expected that it would be. As a broker I'd seen hundreds of guys try to leave bad situations for either a check from another firm or a better work environment. They've almost always had a chunk ripped out of them on the way out. Firms don't exactly allow you to take your clients and assets with you. Your clients are always called and told about what a loser you are. And it's always the guy you sat next to and ate lunch with every day that makes those calls, the guy who's been to your home and has met your family. Hideous, disgusting culture.

I got out easy. I wasn't going to a rival brokerage firm, and I wasn't recruiting any brokers to come with me, and so the firm gave me a pass. It wouldn't have mattered; I was fighting for my life and for my family, and I would've destroyed anyone who tried to stand in my way.

But I don't think much about those days anymore. It's amazing how you can go through a multiyear ordeal and have its effects on you be washed away so quickly. I know it doesn't work that way for veterans who've seen combat, but my situation was more akin to a stay in prison than a tour of duty on a battlefield. I still have the scars but no lasting emotional damage that I'm aware of.

I'd spent my entire adult life in the most brutal business you can do while wearing a white collar. I walked away without a single regulatory problem or customer complaint. I felt like an X-wing fighter pilot speeding away as the Death Star imploded in my rearview mirror.

In Somerset Maugham's *The Moon and Sixpence*, we learn that before he was one of the greatest painters in art history, Eugène-Henri-Paul Gauguin was chained to a job he hated as a stockbroker on the Parisian exchange. One day in 1883 he came home and announced to his wife that he had resigned his position at the stock exchange and would pursue painting full time.

It only took two years for the Gauguin family to become both penniless and homeless.

Gauguin would ultimately find what he was looking for on the beaches of Tahiti, in exile from his family, surrounded by nude models and painted canvases. While my story runs partially parallel to his, Tahiti was never an option for me.

At this point I've shoveled so much dirt on Old Wall Street that you may be wondering what it is that I actually do. I'll answer that by telling you that these days I do what I *should* do, not what I *have* to do. My official designation is *investment advisor representative*, and my firm is a *RIA*. And while I have the increased fiduciary responsibility that comes with being an advisor, I feel great about my work and my purpose each day. Not everything goes right; the markets are here to frustrate the maximum amount of people at all times, after all. But most things do go right, and when they don't, they can be fixed. And I work with smart people who are more concerned with what's right rather than "What can I sell?"

I don't receive compensation from any products or syndicates. There are no selling concessions or commissions or transaction fees or ulterior motives or conflicts or special incentives. Only the clients pay me, and the only side of the table I sit on is theirs. And if I'm ever told that it cannot be this way, then I'll quit. I'll never work for anyone but my clients in this business again.

The story of my escape is being repeated all around us. As you read this, there are brokers from every corner of the nation who are having a eureka moment of their own and planning their escape out. The statistics are mind-boggling; it is nothing short of a revolution out there.

The research firm Discovery put out a report in February 2010 that out of over 8,000 wirehouse advisors who had left their jobs in the prior year, 28 percent opted to go independent and only 23 percent joined another wirehouse. While the 28 percent that left traditional firms entirely represents less than a third, consider that only 7 percent of jumping wirehouse advisors had gone the independent route the year before—and so we're talking about a quadrupling over 12 months.

Fidelity Investments is one of the custody firms benefiting from the breakaway broker trend. In a June 2011 survey, Fidelity found that breakaways were "growing their advisory shops at breakneck speed." It found that although breakaways had on average only been in business 11 years versus 14 years for traditional brokers, their assets under management were now higher—$243 million versus $231 million. It also found that breakaways were growing their practices at a significantly higher rate than brokerage firm advisors and were attracting twice as many new clients with portfolios of $5 million and higher.

Maryland-based Willis Consulting puts our ranks in the RIA channel at 110,000 and growing. This is versus the 38,000 that LPL Financial counted in 2005. It's an avalanche. Not a day goes by when I don't see an article in the trade magazines about another high-profile team going independent, despite the enticements dangled before the team by the mother ship.

In the aftermath of the credit crisis, the wirehouses moved aggressively to lock up top producers with record-breaking retention packages, some as high as 300 percent of a rep's trailing 12-month production numbers. All of a sudden and for the first time in decades, the wealth management guys within these firms found themselves as the belles of the ball, now that banking and trading had almost ruined the franchise. Wall Street banks began to prize their consistent asset management divisions. James Gorman, the CEO of Morgan Stanley, mentioned his financial advisors as the firm's bright spot during a CNBC interview from Davos, a forum that had previously been reserved for investment banker worship. In fact, Gorman doubled down on his advisor business with a purchase of a controlling stake in Smith Barney from the capsizing Citigroup.

But those incredibly generous retention packages and lockups are now coming up on expiration, and it remains to be seen how many of the brokers re-up. Of the brokers that don't, some will simply move from one wirehouse to another for a bigger check. In the industry, we call this a "prisoner exchange." No matter what, the smart money would bet that many of these brokers and advisor teams will be striking out on their own and saying no to the check in exchange for the same freedom that I have found. How many old-school Merrill guys really want to spend the rest of their careers selling Bank of America mortgages and insurance products?

Technology has played a huge role in the mass exodus from brokerage firms to independent advisory practices. You no longer need to be aligned with a major firm to have access to the most cutting-edge tools and practice management capabilities. In fact, many independent advisors are at a technological advantage to their brokerage firm counterparts these days because of their willingness to try new approaches.

Another driver of the trend is the horrendous abuse that the large firms have put their own reputations through. It used to be that the mere mention of one of these firms was enough for a potential client to write a check. This is no longer the case. Merrill Lynch lost $40 billion or so *of its own money* in 2008, and it wants to manage yours? An old Jewish proverb asks, "Would you bring your shoes to the village cobbler if his children were roaming about the streets barefoot?" Wachovia (now Wells Fargo) was no better, nor was Smith Barney or Morgan Stanley or Citigroup or Bank of America. Bear and Lehman just outright disappeared, although Lehman's asset management subsidiary, Neuberger Berman, actually escaped intact. And as for the reputation of Goldman Sachs Asset Management, let's just say it's not a good look to have your parent company scolded in the Senate for screwing over half the clients in favor of the other half.

These fading giants can spend as much money as they like on image and branding; people don't care anymore, and no one is fooled. A recent survey ranked the large banks in lower esteem than tobacco companies and airlines among ordinary Americans.

Being an independent carries its own set of risks and challenges. Real estate costs money, as does software and health care and marketing and licensing and registration and support staff and compliance and research. But at a certain threshold of assets under management, these items are well worth paying for when an advisor reaches the point where he or she has had enough of the brokerage game.

I reached this point the hard way and much later in my career than I should have. But the important thing is that I reached it and came through to the other side. I can look at myself in the mirror again and smile when I come home to my family, even after the roughest days at the office.

I have broken away, and I've left all the baggage behind. And as promised, everything's going to be OK from now on.

Acknowledgments

The director Elia Kazan once said of playwright Arthur Miller that he "didn't write *Death of a Salesman*. He released it. It was there inside him, waiting to be turned loose. That's the measure of its merit."

At the risk of drawing an unearned comparison, I hope that this book, my first, leaves readers with the same impression. While a rock quarry's worth of research was chipped away at in the formulation of this work, much of the narrative has been trapped inside me awaiting release since the beginning of my career. I am grateful first and foremost to McGraw-Hill for opening up the valve and providing that built-up pressure a means of escape.

I had more help and support from friends, family, and colleagues during the writing of this book than I probably deserved.

I'd first like to thank Alice Cherry at Standard & Poor's for turning over my rock and sending the fateful introductory e-mail that would eventually lead to this book. Thank you to Stephanie Frehrich for bringing this ship to shore, to Janice Race for her endless patience with me, and to everyone at McGraw-Hill for all the support and tolerance of profanity.

I'd also like to thank Ben and Eileen Aronson for the beautiful paintings they so graciously made available for the cover art. Thank you, guys!

My friends and partners at StockTwits are a big reason for why my writing and commentary have found the audience that they have. Thanks to Phil Pearlman, Howard Lindzon, and Justin Paterno and all of StockTwits Nation for giving me that piece of the stage and for continuing to point the spotlight on it; love you, guys.

Thank you to the entire financial blogosphere that accepted me from the beginning and came back to my posts enough to keep me going. Every morning when I log in and begin to post, it is all *for* you and *because of* you. Keep reading please; it means the world to me.

I also want to thank my editors, partners, and friends in the mainstream media. Most especially, I'd like to thank the *Wall Street Journal*'s Thomas Coyle and Kevin Noblet for their patience and encouragement with my contributions. Thanks to *Forbes* for granting me my column and everyone at Yahoo! Finance for having me on set to express my views. Also, John Melloy and Kevin Flynn at CNBC and Paul LaMonica at CNN, I appreciate everything you guys have done for me, truly.

This book featured the ideas and opinions of several friends of mine who've been kind enough to contribute. I'd like to thank Mark Bruno, Tom Brakke, David Merkel, Kristen French, Bill Singer, Carl Richards, Scott Bell, Charles Rotblut, and Jason Zweig for lending their wisdom to the project and helping me broaden the discussion.

To my idol and mentor Barry Ritholtz . . . I really wouldn't know where to begin. Everything I do is an attempt to follow in your footsteps—on the Web, in the markets, and in this book.

To my parents, Linda and Larry and Susan and Harry, there aren't words enough to express my gratitude. Thanks for not giving up on me.

And to my wife and high school sweetheart, Shari, with whom I've spent half my life so far, let me just say *Sine te nihil sum.*

Lastly, a thank you to the investment business for making satire and muckraking come so easily.

INDEX

About the Author

Joshua M. Brown is the vice president of investments at Fusion Analytics Investment Partners and the author of the popular blog *TheReformedBroker.com*. He is also a Forbes.com columnist and a contributor to the *Wall Street Journal* and *StockTwits*. In addition, Brown is frequently quoted by and featured on CNBC, Dow Jones, CNN, Marketplace Radio, AOL, Reuters, the *Financial Times*, the *New York Times*, *Crain's*, *Bloomberg*, and *Fortune*. He lives on Long Island, New York.